Managing Staff Development Programs in Human Service Agencies

Managing Staff Development Programs in Human Service Agencies

Michael J. Austin
Diane Brannon
Peter J. Pecora

Nelson-Hall Publishers nh Chicago

Library of Congress in Publication Data

Austin, Michael J.
  Managing staff development programs in human service
agencies.

  Bibliography: p.
  1. Social workers—In-service training—United States.
2. Social work administration—United States. I. Brannon,
Diane. II. Pecora, Peter J. III. Title.
HV91.A93   1984   361.3'068'3   84-6887
ISBN 0-8304-1104-6 (cloth)
ISBN 0-88229-823-2 (paper)

Manufactured in the United States of America

10 9 8 7 6 5 4 3 2 1

The paper in this book is pH neutral (acid-free).

Contents

Figures

Tables

Preface

STAFF DEVELOPMENT PROGRAMS CAN BE VIEWED FROM many different vantage points. A program could be a single training event or a six-month in-service series of events. Several programs might be the components of an agency's annual salary development plan. For workers, a staff development program might provide opportunities to improve skills and gain new knowledge away from the job. For supervisors, staff development programs may provide an opportunity to improve their own knowledge and skills as well as the capacities of their supervisees. For administrators, agency staff development programs may be viewed as costly enterprises and justifiable only in terms of disseminating new agency policies and procedures. From the perspective of service recipients, staff development programs may be seen as essential if clients are to be served by staff who are up-to-date and knowledgeable about new treatment or service-delivery approaches.

These multiple perspectives raise a number of interesting questions: (1) Can staff development programs meet the needs of different constituencies? (2) To what extent do the various views of staff development contribute to covering up or masking the need for reorganizing agency functions and programs? (3) To what extent is the issue of staff development confused when it is viewed primarily in terms of a job or staff person rather than as an agency function shared by all levels of staff? The answers to these questions are both simple and complex. First of all, well-planned staff development programs can meet the needs of different constituents. While the planning process may be viewed as complex, the ingredients of the process are described in much detail in subsequent chapters. Second, the different views of staff development may contribute to masking the need to reorganize an agency in terms of reassigning authority and responsibilities. However, an agency staff development plan that identifies training needs related to organizational factors as well as training needs related to individual staff members can help to place sensitive issues on the table for discussion and action. And third, the staff development function in many agencies is confused when viewed in terms of one person's job (e.g., staff development specialist). This book is based on the premise that staff development management functions can be performed by a committee of staff members, by staff members whose job descriptions reflect duties related to staff development, or a staff member whose full-time responsibilities relate to staff development program management. Irrespective of the agency's staffing pattern, it is clear that all levels of staff, especially top-level administration, need to support and participate in the staff development function.

The different perspectives suggest the need for a working definition of staff development management, and the following statement reflects our best effort. Staff development program management includes:

(1) scanning the environment for social policies and innovations that could influence the service delivery and administrative functions of agency personnel,

(2) analyzing the agency as an organization for issues and/or problems that affect either the delivery of services or the administrative supports of such services,

(3) assessing the training needs of all staff, and

(4) planning, managing, and evaluating programs that are based on the integration of the data that was gathered from the scanning, analyzing, and assessing activities.

Why is staff development program management so important in the 1980s and 1990s? The recent efforts on the part of federal, state, and local governments to control the growth of social welfare expenditures signals an important shift in societal priorities. Irrespective of one's view of this shift, it has become increasingly clear that the service and entitlement dollars will be rationed. Since a large portion of public and voluntary agency budgets is devoted to personnel costs, it is clear that efforts will be made to ration these costs by asking staff to do more with fewer resources.

One rationed resource will be annual salary increments. While such rationing is deplorable in the light of the relatively low salaries paid in the social welfare field, it appears that *creative staff development program management could become the new fringe benefit for the 1980s and 1990s*. One example of such creativity can be seen in the recent settlement of the strike between the communications workers and our largest telephone company. On-the-job training (usually reserved for job entry) was redefined to include ongoing training in areas outside of one's immediate job responsibilities in order to enhance the worker's capacity to survive job reassignments within the company and/or to be competitive in the job market in the event that the company no longer needed the worker's services. This is an example of the commitment of an organization's management and labor to provide opportunities for employees *to grow*. A similar effort has been underway for the past few years with the development of quality circles as an example of an organization's commitment to provide employees with an opportunity *to participate in decision making.* Why should nonprofit human service agencies be any less committed to staff development opportunities than is the for-profit sector? Some would argue that the very nature of a human service agency dictates that the provision of humane client services begins with the humane treatment of all levels of human service agency personnel.

Based on observations and participation in the staff development programs of public and voluntary human service agencies, we have engaged in a collaborative effort to define and describe the management issues confronting agency staff development programs. We have organized our thoughts in response to several questions, and we began by developing a framework for viewing staff development program management in the form of six questions. Our goal was to create a model of proactive staff development management. Each chapter addresses one of the six major questions.

Chapter 1 deals with the interaction between social policies and staff development programs. This chapter describes the process by which policy developments and changes in service directives affect staff development planning and, conversely, how training supports the implementation of social policy. In order to identify staff development implications, a policy analysis framework is presented and illustrated with a case example based on the Adoption Assistance and Child Welfare Act of 1980.

In chapter 2, organizational factors are related to staff development planning. Training can serve as the important link between furthering an agency's mission and empowering workers to refine the skills needed to address that mission. Attention is also given to the effects of organizational structure, process, and environment on the agency's staff development needs and resources. A format for combining such needs and resources into a written staff development plan is included.

Chapter 3 emphasizes the individual worker's perspective on staff development programs. The roles of the worker as a self-actualizing human being, as a professional or paraprofessional with career development interests, and as an organizational member are described in order to identify their implications for staff development program management.

Chapter 4 includes a description of alternative methods for conducting training-needs assessments. A variety of organization-based and worker-based methods are described and assessed. Methods for gathering, analyzing, and presenting assessment data are illustrated with examples.

Chapter 5 addresses the instructional functions of staff development management. The staff development manager or committee can serve as translator of training needs into learning objectives, orchestrator of training events, learning group facilitator, and finally as change agent in relation to individuals and the organization.

Finally, chapter 6 describes alternative methods of evaluating the impact of training programs. Evaluation skills are an essential part of proactive staff development management. Several methods for conducting both process and outcome evaluations are illustrated with examples.

While we assume full responsibility for the content, we wish to acknowledge the contribution of the following colleagues: Art Dodson, Howard Doueck, Nancy Dickinson, Sally Graves, Ronald Green, Helen

Ormsby, Jim Green, Floyd Bolitho, Patricia Anthony, Michael Auch, Arlene Brex, Shirley Carey, Leslie Carlson, Sally Carlson, Ross Cusack, Vikki Dehmen, Kim Dematteo, Virginia Fredericks, Victoria Gawlik, Lori Gradinger, Cynthis Guartney, Joni Hardcastle, Rawleigh Irwin, Ernie Jones, Jo King, Kari Knutson, Frances Leary, Theresa Marquez, Judy Martin, Les McCabe, Diane Mercer, Dave Nichols, Gena Palm, Davida Puesley, Pauline Rose, Margaret Schonfield, Marie Valenzuela, and Steve Wilson. The consultation of Ruth Salinger, James Mosel, and Mark Zober regarding the PAPA approach is most appreciated. Additionally, we acknowledge the support of the Northwest Regional Child Welfare Training Center (OHDS/ACYF 90CT 1954/3) and the Center for Social Welfare Research at the University of Washington School of Social Work.

Michael J. Austin
Seattle, Washington

Diane Brannon
Lawrence, Kansas

Peter J. Pecora
Salt Lake City, Utah

Introduction

WHILE MUCH OF THE STAFF TRAINING AND DEVELOPMENT literature reflects a heavy emphasis on instructional techniques and participant involvement, very little attention has been given to the principles and practices of managing a staff development program in a human service agency. A systems perspective is useful for understanding the management components of the staff development process: (1) analyzing social policies relevant to the agency's mission; (2) incorporating organizational and worker perspectives; (3) assessing worker learning needs; (4) designing training events; and (5) evaluating training activities.

The staff development function can be defined as the orienting, updating, and upgrading of agency personnel in order to provide the highest quality of services to clients. This function can be assumed by many different people in an agency. In some agencies, full-time staff development personnel assume responsibility for managing this function. In other agencies, a senior staff member incorporates part-time staff development functions into his or her overall job requirements. In yet other agencies, staff development responsibilities are delegated to a staff committee for design and implementation. Even when none of these arrangements exists in an agency, supervisory personnel assume some responsibility for the staff development of their subordinates. And finally, in agencies with a flat hierarchical structure and team delivered services, individual staff members assume considerable responsibility for their own ongoing professional development.

The design and implementation of staff development programs will obviously vary according to its location in the hierarchy of the organization. Staff development specialists working full-time or part-time, usually under the supervision of the agency director or program chief, will usually reflect a strong *agency* orientation to the staff development process. In contrast, as one moves down the organizational chart, where staff committees, supervisors, and individual staff members assume responsibility for staff development, training goals and objectives are more likely to reflect a stronger *worker* orientation to staff development.

Both the agency and the worker orientation to the staff development function are critical components of the framework utilized in developing this book. Figure I.1 reflects these components in the format of key questions and activities for persons performing the functions of a staff development manager. The goal of the following discussion is to describe the key questions.

How Do Social Policies and Service Directives Relate to Agency Staff Development Programs?

The first component includes an analysis of current social policies affecting the agency. Social policies may emanate from federal, state, or local legislative bodies or from the decision-making process of the boards of directors that govern voluntary social agencies. An analysis of current social policy emanating

FIGURE I.1.

The process of managing an agency staff development program.

CHAPTER 1	CHAPTER 2	CHAPTERS 3 AND 4	CHAPTER 5	CHAPTER 6
How do social policies and service directives relate to agency staff development programs?	How are organizational factors related to a staff development plan?	How does the agency take into account the worker's view of staff development programs?	How do trainers plan and implement a training event?	How do trainers evaluate training events?
Social policy analysis	Assessing the agency's mission	Assessing personal, professional, and organizational perspectives	Designing instructional process and content	Assessing acquisition of new knowledge and skills
Assessing policy implementation requirements	Assessing the agency's structure, processes, and environment	Assessing the training needs of workers	Selecting a variety of learning experiences	Assessing changes in worker attitudes
Specifying training implications	Developing an agency staff development plan	Transforming needs assessment data into learning objectives	Assessing learner readiness	Assessing relationship between increased worker competence and improved client outcomes

from governmental or other sources can provide the staff development manager with insight into the specific ideas or intentions of the policymakers in seeking to change and improve services to clients.

In addition to the analysis of social policies, staff development specialists need to analyze new service delivery approaches described at conferences, reflected in recent journals and books, or described in reports on research and demonstration projects for staff development program implications. Assessing the feasibility of implementing new service delivery approaches is another management function of a staff development manager, who should continuously monitor changes for their training implications. '

The skills in policy analysis and assessing policy implementation include maintaining a current knowledge of relevant journal and text literature as well as a capacity to anticipate and evaluate legislation in order to identify training implications. In summary, these analytic skills require a systems perspective that seeks to relate changing social policies, emerging trends, new service innovations, and recent research findings to the ongoing life of the agency's staff.

How Are Organizational Factors Related to a Staff Development Plan?

One of the primary activities of agency administrators is translating social policy or legislation into service directives, usually found in administrative guidelines or procedures. The second component of the model requires the staff development manager, with other managers, to interpret service directives in the light of the organization's structure and processes for relevant staff development implications. This analytic process includes the assessment of the organization's mission, its structure and internal processes, and its environmental context. Such analysis enables the staff development manager to incorporate new training activities into the agency's staff development plan, specify the limitations of training, and thereby articulate the implications of the new service directives that cannot be successfully addressed through staff development.

Two examples can illustrate the analytic activities. First, a state mental health agency seeking to implement a new law passed by the legislature related to serving the chronically mentally ill should identify the specific service directives necessary to implement a new policy, as well as the related need for staff orientation and training. Then the staff development manager or committee, in collaboration with the agency administrator, should identify the staff development implications of the new policy in reference to the agency's goals, its current organizational structure and processes, and the environmental context from which the policy emerged. For example, if a policy change requires major changes in job responsibilities and the personnel system is controlled by rigid civil service requirements, training programs may prove to be the critical vehicle for promoting organizational change.

Second, these policy analysis activities can also be carried out in relationship to new service innovations. The experiences of William Glaser in treating troubled adolescents with the technique of reality therapy, reported in journals and books, could be assessed from the perspective of how staff trained to use such a technique might also require changes in service programs. In such a case, careful consideration needs to be given to organizational climate, service standards, the staff development plan, and the limitations of retraining staff.

Assessing how organizational factors relate to the staff development plan also requires the use of skills in the areas of organizational analysis, job analysis, and staff development planning. The organizational analysis skills include the ability to analyze (1) the way in which the agency's structure and function affect workers and (2) the role of organizational performance factors such as productivity, workload demands, worker morale, staff communication, and program coordination. Job analysis involves the assessment of current job descriptions in order to determine how much of a change will be needed in current work routines to accommodate the new service directives. Specific planning skills are needed to develop the following components of an agency's staff development plan: (1) a description of the purpose, goals, and objectives of the agency or program, (2) service delivery priorities from both the management and worker perspectives, (3) policies and procedures for orienting, updating, and upgrading all levels of staff, (4) mechanisms for periodic training needs assessment and training evaluation, and (5) a timetable specifying action plans to be carried out by staff development personnel and/or training committees. All of these components are necessary for implementing a successful staff development program.

How Does the Agency Take into Account the Views of Workers?

The third component of the systems model involves an analysis of worker views of staff development as well as the assessment of worker training needs. The activities of analysis and assessment are formal and informal. The informal process may include assisting a group of program managers, supervisors, and representatives of direct service staff in gaining input from all levels of the organization and translating multiple perceptions into staff development program implications. These implications serve as the basis for developing learning objectives and identifying job specific knowledge, skills, and attitudes. This informal assessment process is frequently omitted, thereby causing much confusion among those ultimately responsible for carrying out training activities.

The formal processes for answering the third question in the model require beginning research skills in conducting training needs assessments that seek to monitor the changing career and service delivery needs of staff. These skills include designing or modifying needs assessment questionnaires, developing interview schedules, analyzing quality control and/or quality assurance reports in order to identify staff development implications, and incorporating the training needs assessment process into the ongoing routines of the agencies (e.g., sending out the questionnaire on a semiannual basis along with the payroll checks.)

With the written results of the group process and/ or training needs assessment, the staff development manager is in a position to seek outside consultation from subject matter experts on potential training resources. Such consultation could focus on: (1) using agency staff experts, (2) using outside training experts, (3) defining the different training techniques most relevant to each learning objective, and/or (4) the availability of relevant literature. With ideas in all of these areas, the instructional design and implementation phase can begin.

How Do Trainers Plan and Implement a Training Event?

The fourth component of the model is instructional design and implementation. This component includes (1) specifying the knowledge content, the skills to be acquired, and the attitudes to be encouraged in relationship to job requirements and worker performance; (2) the learning methods and experiences to be utilized; and (3) an assessment of learner readiness as reflected in worker experience, morale, and workload demands. Instructional design is more than planning exercises, distributing reading materials, and arranging for training sites. It needs to include an assessment of the existing knowledge and skills possessed by the potential participants as well as an assessment of the organizational climate in which the training will be reinforced or ignored.

All instructional design as well as evaluation activities need to be conducted with the concept of *"andragogy"* or *adult learning* in mind. This concept suggests that adults are generally independent, self-motivated learners whose experience orients them to practical issues. As Knowles (1978) has observed:

1. Adults are motivated to learn as they experience needs and interests that learning will satisfy; therefore, these needs and interests are appropriate starting points for organizing adult learning activities.
2. Adult orientation to learning is life-centered; therefore, the

appropriate units for organizing adult learning are life situations, not subjects.

3. Experience is the richest resource for adult learning; therefore, the core methodology of adult education is the analysis of experience.
4. Adults have a deep need to be self-directing; therefore, the role of the teacher is to engage in a process of mutual inquiry rather than to transmit knowledge to them and then evaluate their conformity to it.
5. Individual differences among people increase with age; therefore, adult education must make optimal provision for differences in style, time, place, and pace of learning.

[P. 31]

It is also important to recognize the process by which staff members return from training experiences to their jobs. We need to identify ways in which new learning will be utilized back on the job. In addition, the implementation of job-relevant training might be carried out by one or more of the following: (1) the staff development specialist, (2) outside experts, (3) agency staff experts, and/or (4) participant expertise. The use of participant expertise is another example of andragogy in that the training event may build upon the expertise of the participants. A training program might be conducted within the agency or contracted out to a university continuing education program or private training organizations or consultants.

The relevant steps for addressing this component of the model include: (1) researching relevant reading materials, (2) planning and implementing learning exercises, simulations, and related experiences, (3) organizing and scheduling the training site, (4) securing the necessary financial and human resources, (5) securing the necessary staff support needed to help newly trained staff use their knowledge and skills back on the job, and (6) marketing the training program.

How Do Trainers Evaluate the Impact of Training Events?

The fifth and final component of the model is training evaluation. This component includes process evaluation (Did they learn what we sought to teach them?) and outcome evaluation (Did the training experience lead to increased worker competence and improved client services?). The process evaluation seeks to measure the nature and amount of knowledge acquired as well as the new learned behaviors related to skill development. In addition, attitude change or reinforcement may also be included in process evaluation.

Outcome evaluation seeks to assess increased worker competence back on the job as well as the barriers that may exist in applying new learning. These barriers may be personal, interpersonal, and/or organizational. Outcome evaluation measures can be used in advance of the training experience in order to develop baseline information against which to measure future change after the training has taken place. In order to make the difficult link between improved worker competence and improved client services, a similar pre- and post-measurement design can be used for specifying the quality of service delivered before and after the training.

Training evaluation, like program evaluation, requires skills in designing instruments to assess the acquisition of new knowledge and skills (e.g., pre- and post-tests, behavioral rating schedules, and attitude change inventories). A variety of methods for acquiring feedback about the training sessions are necessary in order to make improvements in the structure and function of future sessions.

In summary, the questions that comprise the model used in this book are based on the assumption that agency staff development programs require planning and management skills. In the next section, special emphasis is given to identifying the key management roles and techniques needed to guide a staff development program.

The Trainer as Administrator

As an administrator, a trainer or staff development manager needs to be guided by an understanding of the role of staff development in the delivery of social services as well as managerial knowledge and skill required for effective job performance. Some of the managerial skills include: (1) providing and receiving consultation, (2) mobilizing agency and community resources, (3) reaching out to supervisors as supporters and information sources, (4) guiding the agency's staff development committee, and (5) promoting an effective learning environment. The major components of staff development programs include learning activities to orient, update, and upgrade all levels of personnel in order to provide effective and efficient social services to clients. The challenge for the trainer is to maintain a balanced perspective between the needs of workers and the needs of the agency and to recognize that these needs are frequently not the same. Agency needs for staff training may relate to interunit communication, community relations, increased effectiveness, improved efficiency, and program accountability. The goal of this section is to introduce the managerial roles of analyst, planner, program designer, implementor, and evaluator. Subsequent chapters will illustrate the roles in relation to the implementation of a staff development program.

Analyst

The trainer needs to perform the analyst role in order to assess the internal and external agency environment for the purpose of setting staff development priorities. At least four perspectives need to be analyzed: (1) staff defined training needs and interests; (2) agency or top management defined training needs and interests; (3) assessing agency functioning through the identification of organizational development needs; and (4) assessing readiness for agency and worker change through problem-focused conferences or awareness-raising workshops. The trainer who utilizes the analyst role is constantly in search of the following data: (1) currency and relevance of job description data for appropriate performance evaluation and career planning; (2) training needs assessment data; (3) policy data which results in new service directives; (4) research data about innovative service delivery programs and techniques; and (5) organizational performance data reflected in quality control or assurance reports and in informal hallway and coffee room discussions about agency operations and practices. The purpose of collecting a wide variety of data is to develop a systematic overview of all relevant agency activities in order to engage in staff development planning. The data need to be synthesized for presentation to top management and/or a staff development committee for decision making. The analyst role is further described in chapter 2.

Planner

The planning role involves interactional and analytic tasks. The planning model presented in figure I.2 includes five components: (1) defining the problem, (2) building a structure of relationships, (3) formulating objectives and strategies, (4) implementing a program, and (5) monitoring and evaluation (Lauffer, 1978). Clearly the first part of this planning process overlaps with the analyst role and with some of the other roles to be described.

In addition to defining the problem and building a structure, it is important to identify the training program best suited to address the problem. Figure I.3 includes a list of options which the trainer should consider when assuming the planner role.

One of the key aspects of the planner role is mobilizing resources inside and outside the agency. Lauffer (1978) identifies collaborative and strategic resources. Collaborative resources represent the joint use of training programs offered by other agencies, staff use of university continuing education resources that meet the needs of individuals and/or the agency, joint development of training programs with other agencies or professional organizations, and use of staff expertise located elsewhere in the agency, in another agency, in the community, or elsewhere in the state, region, or county. Planning strategies and tactics are needed to make full use of such collaborative resources as facilities, money, personnel, political influence, legitimacy, popularity, and human energy. It is possible to map collaborative resources as in the example of a mental health staff development committee noted in figure I.4.

While mapping resources is the first step in mobi-

FIGURE I.2.
Trainer as planner.

STAGE OR PHASE	ANALYTICAL TASKS	INTERACTIONAL TASKS
1. Identifying the problem. Assessing needs and interests	Studying and describing a situation in preliminary terms: conceptualizing the problem. Assessing what opportunities and limits are set by the resources available, the interests and needs of the consumer population, etc	Receiving and/or eliciting information from those who might serve as sponsors or cosponsors, actual or potential consumers, and other relevant parties
2. Building a structure or network of relationships	Identifying the various actors who should somehow be involved in the program developmentation phases; thinking through a means of communicating with them and the types of structures through which they might be involved. Identifying people for roles as experts, communicators, influencers, etc	Establishing formal and informal communication processes in task forces or planning committees, recruiting participants and helping them to select their roles, and establishing linkages with cooperating bodies or individuals
3. Formulating objectives and intervention strategies	Analyzing past efforts to deal with the problem, thinking through those objectives that seem feasible or operational, examining the resources required to accomplish them, weighing the costs and benefits of one approach over another, and selecting from among them	Promoting expression of opinions and exchange of ideas, testing out the feasibilities of various alternatives with relevant actors, and assisting decision makers to weigh alternatives and overcome resistances to implementation
4. Implementing the program	Working out the logistics of implementation in detail, specifying tasks to be performed and who will be performing them, and estimating costs	Conducting the continuing education activity, e.g., assessment, consultation, training, etc

FIGURE I.2. (*continued*).

| 5. Monitoring and evaluating it | Designing a system for collecting feedback and analyzing information on operations and on accomplishments. Analyzing consequences of actions and possible change, adjustments needed, and new problems that call for action or new program development | Obtaining data from designated sources, and receiving or eliciting information based on the experience of learners and other relevant actors. Communicating findings and recommendations to appropriate persons, consumers, auspice providers, and other interested parties |

SOURCE: From *Doing Continuing Education and Staff Development* by Armand Lauffer (New York: McGraw-Hill, 1978), p. 25. Reprinted by permission.

lizing resources, the securing of staff cooperation inside and outside the agency also requires considerable skill and planning. Within the agency, support may be needed from the director and board as well as from the business office. Outside the agency there may be considerable ambivalence among agencies in sharing resources in a competitive environment or gaining support in a climate of widely divergent training needs. Inadequate effort and attention is usually given to interagency collaboration and, in fact, there may be a reservoir of goodwill for collaboration that far exceeds anyone's expectations. In any event, the needs of agencies are constantly changing. When competition for clients and resources is intense, joint training efforts provide relatively neutral ground for interagency communication. Since agency receptivity for collaboration may be absent at one point in time and present at another point in time, the planner role is a critical, ongoing function.

FIGURE I.3.
Planning options for staff development programs.

SEMINAR
: Usually one instructor
10 to 25 participants
Classroom "teaching" format
"Think tank"—intense exchange on specialized area
Can be "packaged" and repeated

WORKSHOP
: Usually one or two instructors
10 to 75 participants
"Laboratory" style of teaching
Involvement in learning activity
In small group
Can be "packaged" and repeated

CONFERENCE
: Usually many different speakers
50 to 1,000 participants (or more)
A one-time only event usually with meals and parties
Timely with updates on new legislation and/or skills
Group cohesion around issue or action
Often a group with members belonging to same organization
Pass resolutions/issue press releases

INSTITUTE/
SYMPOSIUM
: Usually 5 to 50 speakers
50 to 500 participants
Often addressing a new service innovation or set of skills
Demonstration of service outcomes
Participants are "fed" lots of information
Not much group interaction
"Formal" structure

BRIEFING
: Usually one presenter
One theme
Usually half-day or less
Selected audience—"leaders" or specific group
Many handout materials

COLLOQUIUM
: Usually one presenter
1 to 2 hours (less than half day)
Presentation of research or service innovation
Questions from participants

FIGURE I.3. (*continued*).

FORUM   Panel of "experts" delivers information
50 to 200 participants
Focus on a public issue/problem
Cross-section of community
Audience reaction and feedback

Program designer

The development of a staff development program should obviously relate to the data compiled as part of the analyst role and staff input gained as part of the planner role. Program design requires continuity, sequencing, and integration (Tyler, 1950). *Continuity* involves the recognition that staff development activities are part of a larger system and that previous staff experiences need to be linked in a continuous fashion with the actual training experience and future experiences or training. For example, a staff development program can be spread out over time, such as a two-day workshop followed three months later with a one-day session to allow for job application of the training content. Continuity also accounts for such staff differences as personalities, prior education, prior work experience, and career interests.

Sequencing refers to the manner by which individual learning activities are organized in relationship to the personal interests, needs, and capacities of staff to be trained. The trainer shares the responsibility for sequential learning with the trainees by conscious attention to building new ideas and information upon previous experiences (e.g., eliciting examples of personal experiences) and reinforcing learning by generalizing

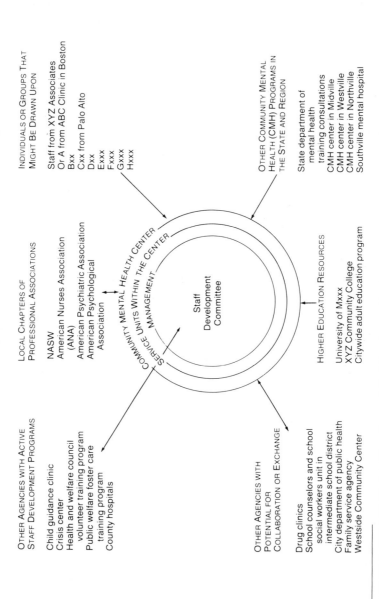

FIGURE I.4. *Sample collaborative resources inventory.*

OTHER AGENCIES WITH ACTIVE STAFF DEVELOPMENT PROGRAMS

Child guidance clinic
Crisis center
Health and welfare council
Public welfare foster care
  volunteer training program
  training program
County hospitals

LOCAL CHAPTERS OF PROFESSIONAL ASSOCIATIONS

NASW
American Nurses Association (ANA)
American Psychiatric Association
American Psychological Association

INDIVIDUALS OR GROUPS THAT MIGHT BE DRAWN UPON

Staff from XYZ Associates
Or A from ABC Clinic in Boston
Bxx
Cxx from Palo Alto
Dxx
Exxx
Fxxx
Gxxx
Hxxx

OTHER COMMUNITY MENTAL HEALTH (CMH) PROGRAMS IN THE STATE AND REGION

State department of mental health training consultations
CMH center in Midville
CMH center in Westville
CMH center in Northville
Southville mental hospital

COMMUNITY MENTAL HEALTH CENTER
SERVICE UNITS WITHIN THE CENTER
MANAGEMENT

Staff Development Committee

OTHER AGENCIES WITH POTENTIAL FOR COLLABORATION OR EXCHANGE

Drug clinics
School counselors and school social workers unit in intermediate school district
City department of public health
Family service agency
Westside Community Center

HIGHER EDUCATION RESOURCES

University of Mxxx
XYZ Community College
Citywide adult education program

SOURCE: From *Doing Continuing Education and Staff Development* by Armand Lauffer (New York: McGraw-Hill, 1978), P. 25. Reprinted by permission.

beyond specific experiences. For example, learning content presented on the first day of a workshop can be reinforced through a learning exercise on the second day and/or participant job experiences can be utilized to shape the direction of a learning exercise. Some trainers organize learning experiences by orienting the learner to the whole idea or experience before focusing on the parts, while other trainers seek to specify the particular parts or skills before moving to general principles or identifying the utility of the parts.

Integration refers to the ability to weave the learning/teaching experience with the worker's job experience into a total fabric. This process of putting it all together in one's mind is enhanced by the trainer's conscious effort to specify how the various components of the training program relate to one another and to the job. For example, seeking participant feedback in a debriefing session will quickly alert the trainer to the different ways in which the training content is being integrated by the participants. Related to the process of integration is Piaget's observation that *the logic of learning is different from the logic of teaching.* Whatever the logic might be for the training program design, the staff to be trained will organize and utilize the learning experiences in a way that usually differs from the continuity, sequencing, and integration intentions of the program designer.

Implementor

This managerial role is characterized by extensive attention to detail. These details include the dissemination of training program announcements, recruiting and screening potential participants, establishing a contract with those doing the instruction if the trainer is not the instructor, locating the training site and arranging for a comfortable environment, ordering and delivering necessary training supplies ranging from name tags to newsprint, and developing and monitoring a staff development program budget. The trainer may manage all these implementation activities or contract with a university continuing education program or private training organization to carry out these activities. See appendix A for an implementor's checklist. Whatever the implementation process, the budget is the key planning and management document.

The most common training program budget is a line-item budget that itemizes the major costs of personnel, consultation, facilities, equipment, supplies, and travel (see figure I.5). Each item needs to be fully described and justified in an accompanying narrative section. Why is equipment needed? What will the consultants be doing? How are travel costs computed? The personnel item includes salary estimates and fringe benefits for all full-time and part-time professional, clerical, and support staff. Consultation costs relate to assistance provided by individuals to the planning, implementation, or evaluation of the training program and are usually computed in terms of hourly or daily fees as well as travel and per diem expenses. Facility costs usually involve training room rentals in hotels or conference centers and are usually based on a daily user fee. Equipment costs can include the rental of audiovisual equipment, telephones, and other training aids. Supply costs usually include office supplies, training materials, printed brochures, media advertisements, and duplicated materials. Travel

FIGURE I.5.
Developing a budget for a training event.

STEP 1: Identify as accurately as possible the following typical costs associated with each part of the program.

1. Honoraria for training event presenters
2. Audiovisual expenses
3. Morning and afternoon coffee expenses including tax and gratuities
4. Advertisement expenses (newspaper, professional newsletters, etc.)
5. Printing and mailing costs for brochures
6. Duplication of training materials for participants
7. Administrative costs for telephone supplies and related expenses
8. Compute unexpected expenses at 10% of total costs, excluding food

STEP 2: Organize budget data in order to compute costs per participant by identifying fixed costs (i.e., costs that remain the same no matter how many participants attend).

Fixed costs for a two-day workshop for 30 participants:

• Honoraria ($500/day for one trainer)	$1,000
• Trainer travel and per diem	300
• Audiovisual equipment rental	50
• Advertisements	75
• Participant coffee ($2/day)	120
• Brochure printing and mailing	350
• Duplication of training materials	100
• Administrative costs	500
• Unexpected costs (10% of $2,495)	250
	$2,825

Cost per participant ($2,825 ÷ 30) = $94

SOURCE: Adapted from Simerly, 1981.

costs generally involve the mileage rate or air travel costs for the instructional staff and the per diem costs of hotel and food that are required for the instructional staff. Sometimes budgets include mileage reimbursement to staff for attending agency-sponsored staff development programs.

Evaluator

The key activity of this managerial role is the design and implementation of a training program evaluation which is described in chapter 6. However, the evaluation process extends across all the managerial roles. The analyst and planner roles involve the evaluation of data and the decision-making process. The program designer and implementor roles include the evaluation of the capacities of the participants, the consultants, the trainers, and the potential for funding.

The evaluation process includes monitoring the way in which the training experience is structured to account for different types of adult learning. In particular, staff development programs need to reflect opportunities for the learner to select from among a number of different learning activities.

The motivation of potential participants is another area for evaluation. While some staff will be highly motivated to participate in a staff development program, others may see themselves as coerced or sent by their supervisor and may become reluctant learners. It is important to assess the value of different training rewards, including certificates, opportunities for career advancement, salary increases, colleague recognition, opportunity to get away from the office, and opportunity to travel to an interesting place inside or outside the state. For some staff, the training experience, the peer interaction, and the knowledge and skills acquired will be the reward. For staff who attend continuing education workshops, the peer contact and new knowledge may also influence career planning and contribute to the realization that a change in jobs is needed.

Since there is a growing recognition that the retention and transfer of the knowledge and skills acquired in training workshops are strengthened when learning occurs in a meaningful training environment, the integrative process of "learning by doing" reflected in experiential training exercises also should be evaluated. It is important to plan for participants to evaluate their own experiential learning in order to see whether or not retention and transfer have been increased. Does the training program encourage participants to become increasingly independent learners in pursuing their own educational agenda? To what extent has the training program heightened personal motivation, intellectual curiosity, sense of creativity, awareness of resources, and capacity to use resources? The evidence for independent learning might be found in special projects completed on the job after a workshop.

In summary, five managerial roles have been described as part of the trainer's administrative functions. In the next two chapters, more attention is given to the role of analyst. However, before describing the management of staff development programs in detail, it might be useful to complete the self-assessment inventory included in Appendix B. While all the items in the inventory will not be addressed in this book, many of them will be discussed.

References

Johnson, D. W., and Johnson, F. P. *Joining Together: Group Theory and Group Skills.* Englewood Cliffs, N.J.: Prentice-Hall, 1975.

Knowles, M. S. *The Modern Practice of Adult Education.* New York: Association Press, 1970.

Lauffer, A. *Doing Continuing Education and Staff Development.* New York: McGraw-Hill, 1978.

Simerly, R. *How to Plan and Administer Successful Budgets for Noncredit Continuing Education Programs.* Champaign: University of Illinois Press, 1981.

Tyler, R. W. *Basic Principles of Curriculum and Instruction: Syllabus for Education 360.* Chicago: University of Chicago Press, 1955.

Chapter 1

How Do Social Policies Relate to Agency Staff Development Programs?

THE ANALYST ROLE OF THE STAFF DEVELOPMENT MANAGER position is not widely recognized. For some people, the analysis of internal organizational data and external social policy information is an intuitive process carried out by staff development personnel with strong management orientations. For others, analyzing such internal and external information is seen as a waste of time with little relevance for staff development programming. This chapter and chapter 2 should make clear that the analysis of social policies and the assessment of organizational factors are essential activities for the effective staff development manager.

The social policies that guide the delivery of social services directly affect and are affected by training and staff development. Staff development managers, therefore, need to be skilled in interpreting the implications of policies in order to develop training programs as well as to anticipate the needs of staff who must implement the social policies. This chapter addresses policy analysis from a staff development perspective and includes an analysis of the federal Adoption Assistance and Child Welfare Act of 1980 (P.L.

96-2727) to illustrate the process of specifying training implications derived from a social policy.

The Linkage Between Policy Implementation and Training

While social policies clearly influence an agency's training priorities, training itself can also influence the agency's implementation of both social and administrative policy. Training is a crucial and usually overlooked link in the policy process. Hargrove (1975) notes that we are more proficient at demonstrating the need for and evaluating the results of policies than we are at implementing them. He suggests the following policy analysis questions that highlight the central role of training in policy implementation:

1. What cooperation inside and outside the agency is likely to be needed for successful policy implementation?
2. Does the implementation of the policy threaten the jobs or status of those who could block implementation?
3. Do existing staff have the professional capabilities to perform the work required?
4. Does the policy require different behavior on the part of staff and how realistic is this?
5. Is there a sufficient range of interventive methods for staff to use in implementing the policy?

Training programs are frequently used as part of the answer to these questions. Since new or changed policies frequently threaten the status quo, the staff development manager needs to engage in systems-oriented policy analysis in order to anticipate where these changes are most likely to be resisted, both within the agency and among the other organizations and individuals in the agency's working environment. Policy analysis is defined here as an accounting process whereby the choices and assumptions underlying existing or proposed policies are made explicit. With such analyses planning can proceed by translating the value choices into concrete programs using available resources and technology.

While staff development managers usually do not have primary responsibility for the agency's policy analysis and planning, it is important that they are familiar with these processes. By engaging in policy analysis and planning, the staff development manager ensures that staff development programs are closely linked to policy implementation and thereby contribute to the goals of the agency. The staff development manager, then, must be able to analyze and interpret policy by addressing many of the following questions (Gil, 1973).

I. General Questions
    1. What client problems are the current or new policies seeking to address?
    2. Is it possible to detect any underlying assumptions about the causes of the client's problems reflected in this policy?
    3. What assumptions does the policy make about the agency and worker's capacities to assist the clients?
    4. What is the administrative, legislative, or judicial history of the policy?

II. Specific Questions
   1. What are the policy objectives and what values underlie the objectives?
   2. What assumptions underlie the service strategies that emerge from the policy objectives?
   3. What are the potential effects of the policy on clients *and* staff (intended effects and unintended effects in the short and long range)?

III. Implications/Questions
   1. How will the policy change the living situation of clients and the work situation of staff?
   2. What new tasks and functions will staff be expected to assume and what current tasks will assume lower priority?
   3. What new rewards and constraints will the policy generate for clients and staff?
   4. What new relationship will staff be expected to develop?
   5. How will the new policy affect the quality of work life for staff?
   6. How might the values underlying the policy conflict with the values and norms of the workers?
   7. What are the intended and unintended consequences of the interaction between the policy and staff morale?

Many of these questions can be answered by analyzing data gathered from memoranda, staff meetings or briefings, newspapers and journals, and person-to-person contacts or networks. It is not enough to wait for information to be routed from the top down or the bottom up. Proactive staff development managers seek out others and develop informed networks to facilitate the flow of policy information. It is also important to be able to sift through volumes of information about policy developments as well as to detect the number of interpretations that have already been made by others who have processed the information.

Since most new social policies are of sufficient scope to have training implications, staff development managers need to communicate regularly with the agency's top administrators. Briefing sessions on new policies need to include projected training implications. If the implications are not identified in advance, staff development managers need to be assertive in alerting top management to the continuous need for assessing the training implications early in the policy implementation process.

In addition to getting the facts about policy developments and the agency executive's interpretation, it is important for staff development managers to have specific knowledge of service programs and staff competencies in order to make a productive link between training needs and policy implementation. The staff development manager also needs to maintain continuous contact with supervisory and line staff in order to (1) gain knowledge about practice realities, (2) acquire information about relevant literature, and (3) collect feedback about the potential impact of implementing a new policy. A sound base of professional knowledge will help prevent dependence on the bandwagon approach to training and the uncritical adoption of well-marketed programs or fads. Such a foundation is essential for making a convincing case for the merits of a comprehensive staff development program. Nothing is more damaging to morale (and the good name of staff development) than to compel workers to attend training on a subject seemingly irrelevant to their jobs and offered by a trainer who lacks the technical information or motivation to be convincing.

In order to assist staff development managers with the policy analysis process, the following guidelines have been designed to help identify information related to policy, practice, and training in public and voluntary agencies:

   I. Analyze the sources of the policy initiative (legislation, hearings, proceedings)
  II. Identify service directives (administrative interpretation of policy initiative)
 III. Assess feasibility of implementing the policy (the views of administrators, supervisory and line staff, and trainees)
 IV. Assess impact on staff job tasks (in collaboration with supervisors and workers)
  V. Specify training implications (for agency administrators, staff development manager, supervisors and workers)
 VI. Identify learning objectives (involving the staff development manager and educational specialist)
VII. Specify training content and format (for staff development manager and/or trainer)

These guidelines are used in a case example described in the next section.

The Case of the Adoption Assistance and Child Welfare Act of 1980

I. *Source of Policy Initiative.* The federal Adoption Assistance and Child Welfare Act of 1980 was based upon the mounting evidence that the foster care system in this country was being abused with over 500,000 children in out-of-home care (Shyne and Shroeder, 1978) along with sufficient evidence from successful demonstration projects that prevention and permanency planning for children was indeed possible. The major policy thrust was to encourage states, with fiscal incentives, to reduce the number of children in foster care. The policy mechanisms for addressing the problem included adoption subsidies for special needs children, improved tracking and review of foster care caseloads, and increased use of preventive services. Additional policy components as identified in the federal regulations for the act included the following:

1. A statewide inventory of children in substitute care by age, race, sex, date/reason/location of placement, and other demographic information.
2. A comprehensive management information system to track children in care.
3. Provision of a range of preventive services such as intensive family counseling, emergency services, and homemaker services.
4. Written case plans listing goals and a timeline for each child in care.
5. Case review consisting of judicial or administrative reviews every six months and a dispositional hearing after eighteen months in care.
6. Provision of restorative services such as intensive family counseling, day care, or respite care.
7. Placement in the least restrictive setting in close proximity to a child's family.
8. Procedural safeguards that mandate court orders for child removal in all but emergency cases and parent/child involvement in case planning.
9. Permanent planning services including use of

guardianship, long-term foster care, and adoption options.

II. *Identifying Service Directives.* In a briefing for managers on the new policy and its effects on the agency, the administrator of a public child welfare agency might identify the following new service directives:

1. Standardized case plans will be submitted and monitored through a centralized information system.
2. No child will be removed from his or her home until a support strategy involving preventive services has been attempted and failed, except in emergency cases.
3. Recruitment for adoptive parents will be expanded to remove traditional restrictions based on marital, health, cultural, or economic status.
4. The continuum of services used to support the maintenance or reunification of families will be expanded to include all those currently available in the community at large.

III. *Assessing Feasibility of Implementing the Policy.* Ideally, the agency administrator has thought through the implications of the new policy by answering the implementation feasibility questions noted at the beginning of this chapter. In this case, let us assume that the only implementation issue raised by the administrator was that the new service directives would serve to complicate the casework process with additional service alternatives, providers, forms, and procedures.

The staff development manager assesses the service directives stated by agency administrators in order to clearly understand the administrator's perspective on the values and issues raised by the policy change. Keenly aware of the fact that policy does not automatically produce procedures and practices, the staff development manager looks at the implementation feasibility questions in relation to each identified service directive. For example, assessing the requirements for a preventive services program offered to families prior to placing a child in foster care using the previously cited implementation questions might yield the following answers:

1. *What cooperation from staff who work inside and outside the agency is likely to be needed for successful implementation?*
   Prevention of out-of-home placement is likely to require involvement of all the institutions and agencies that affect all families as well as those individuals included in that family's informal support networks. Staff will need to identify any new policies and procedures required for involving other agencies.

2. *Does the implementation of the policy threaten the jobs or status of those who could block implementation?*
   The caseworker-as-counselor role will be supplanted by a case manager role, with the worker relinquishing control over many aspects of the helping process in order to involve ''nontraditional'' helpers. This might be viewed as freeing staff to do what they know best by acting as brokers or it may be viewed as an effort by other helpers to take over traditional staff jobs.

3. *Do existing staff have the professional capabilities to perform the work required?*
   Helping families under stress remain intact re-

quires skills in crisis intervention, network management, and creative problem solving, which some workers can demonstrate but others can not.

4. *Does the policy require different behavior on the part of staff, and how realistic is this?*
Caseworkers will need to change the nature of their intervention, focusing more directly on family strengths than on problems. Many staff have little experience in developing behaviorally specific and problem-focused casework objectives. Some staff will find it difficult to formulate case plans oriented toward family welfare since their past orientation has primarily been the welfare of the child.

5. *Is there a sufficient range of interventive methods for staff to use in implementing the policy?*
The technological uncertainties are numerous, most notably that the various intervention techniques and services for helping troubled families in their own homes have not been tested across a broad range of problems and situations.

IV. *Impact on Staff Job Tasks.* Regardless of the clarity of the analysis up to this point, a major effort will usually be required to implement the policy since training implications are rarely specified in the law or regulations. Therefore, the staff development manager must sell the need for training up and down the agency hierarchy, making clear that training must be relevant to the stresses that occur when changes in job behavior are required.

For this reason, it is essential that the staff development manager talk with line staff about how the new service directives will affect their jobs. Line workers may not be in a position to identify the training implications of each service directive, but they can identify the barriers to policy implementation. First line supervisors are also important sources of service delivery information. For example, supervisors might identify the most significant barrier to implementing the law such as locating a range of preventive services in the community and assessing their appropriateness. Alternatively, most line workers may be uncomfortable in having their work scrutinized by periodic monitoring of case plans. Whatever these implementation issues are, they are less likely to be identified by the top administrators than they are by the staff who implement policies. Therefore staff development managers must use their own practice knowledge to interpret the views of supervisors and line workers regarding the impact of policy shifts on agency jobs.

V. *Specifying Training Implications.* After the changes in job behavior are assessed, the staff development manager must unravel the training implications that may range from issues related to organizational structure to needed changes in personnel management. As a third party negotiator between top management and line workers the staff development manager is able to maintain credibility by helping to clarify positions and establish a mutuality of expectations. For example, if case management training emerged as the top priority issue, it would be necessary to link it to the agency's efforts to fund preventive services and the line staff's efforts to implement preventive services. A proactive staff development manager frequently makes recommendations on policy or agency structure and seeks to educate all staff about the problems that are not solvable by training. The manager also needs to alert others about the problems that may impede the effectiveness of training programs designed to promote the implementation of policy directives. For example, neither administrators nor line workers might see the need for case management training. The skilled staff development manager with knowledge of the field, the policy initiatives, and the relevant points of view can exercise an important leadership role by identifying unrecognized training implications and needs.

VI. *Identifying Learning Objectives.* This sifting, sorting, and negotiating process is logically followed by a statement of learning objectives. These objectives are based on the new service directives as interpreted by administrators, current knowledge with regard to managing complex caseloads, and the anticipated effects on job expectations of line staff as well as staff training needs assessment data. The definitions of these learning objectives derive from two questions: What do we want workers to do differently as a result of training? and, How will these changes improve services to clients? At this point the staff development manager may want to consult training specialists in order to specify learning objectives and translate those into training content and formats. While these aspects of the staff development manager's role will be discussed more fully in chapter 4, the following learning objectives might be articulated for the training related to the Adoption Assistance and Child Welfare Act:

1. Upon completion of training focused on utilizing community resources, caseworkers will demonstrate an ability to use a wide range of formal and informal service options.
2. Upon completion of training in case management,

workers will demonstrate the ability to write behaviorally specific case goals which can be evaluated by third party review.

VII. *Specifying Training Content and Format.* The staff development manager or a particular trainer will need to be familiar with relevant professional literature, aware of available expertise, and realistic about agency constraints which may affect the performance of new worker tasks. Training content should reflect the skill level, experience, and orientation of workers. Experienced workers may not need training in community resources. On the other hand, they may be so wedded to traditional service options, like foster care, that they are reluctant to acquire the skills that the new service directives seek to promote. A thorough training needs assessment is essential to informed planning of training content. The choice of training format, whether it be workshops, seminars, one-time discussions in staff meetings, or university continuing education offerings, is often a compromise between the ideal instructional approach and the realities of agency life. Those choices will be discussed in greater detail in chapters 4 and 5.

A well-planned training program is a vital link in an agency's efforts to implement new policies. Policies rarely compel behavior change, though they almost always require it for successful implementation. The staff development manager's responsibilities for identifying training implications and developing programs require soliciting information from top administrators about policy interpretations, from line staff on potential job impact, and from the field of practice (local expertise and professional literature). The synthesis of this information can provide a foundation for a well-conceived training program that serves as a timely and essential support to policy implementation.

References

Gil, D. *Unraveling Social Policy*. Cambridge, Mass.: Schenkman, 1973.

Hargrove, E. *The Missing Link: The Study of Implementation of Social Policy*. Washington, D.C.: Urban Institute, 1975.

Shyne, A. W., and Schroeder, A. G. *National Study of Social Services to Children and Their Families*. Washington, D.C.: U.S. Government Printing Office, 1978. (DHHS Publication No. OHDS 78-3015)

Chapter 2

How Are Organizational Factors Related to Staff Development Planning?

THE PURPOSE OF THIS CHAPTER IS TO EXAMINE THE NA-
ture and consequences of the agency's commitment to
training and staff development. Although the training
and staff development function is clearly a managerial
one, staff development managers often view their location in the organizational hierarchy as a reflection of
the agency's commitment. Is the agency really investing in its human resources through a staff development program or is training used only to retain accred-
itation or maintain appearances by expending the
minimum resources each year to satisfy funding
sources? Increasingly, human service administration
requires efficient use of training resources in order to
develop and enhance agency personnel.

The fundamental purpose of management is to be
able to predict and control human behavior in pursuit
of organizational goals. Staff development programs
are vital to meeting that purpose. The major function
of the staff development manager's role is to ensure
that training resources are used to enhance the agency's mission and its staff's capabilities. Given the goal
of predicting and enhancing staff work behavior, staff
development managers need to be up-to-date on the
capacities and training needs of workers that are related to knowledge, skills, and attitudes. Such information forms the essential ingredients of an agency's

staff development plan. A comprehensive training plan indicates the extent to which training is central to the agency's purposes. The plan also indicates an assessment of worker capabilities and learning interests relative to agency service directives. These data are then meshed to produce training topics, objectives, and formats. To ensure that the plan and its results support the agency's goals, the staff development manager must take into consideration a number of organizational factors. The analysis of an agency requires an understanding of the organization's (1) mission, (2) structure and internal processes, and (3) environmental context. These three factors provide a framework for analyzing an agency's commitment to staff development and a tool for proactive management of staff development.

This framework for analysis includes two well-documented assumptions. First, human beings are constantly learning and developing throughout their lifespan. Organizations invest in staff development programs in order to influence *what* and *how* organization members learn. An extremely laissez-faire management would allow workers to develop without guidance, thereby developing as individuals but not necessarily as organization members. Most enlightened managers seek to enhance worker development by stressing the value of life-long learning. Second, organizations can, to a limited extent, control individual decision making by controlling the flow of information (March and Simon, 1958). Information is usually sorted, simplified, and distributed according to stated and unstated procedures based on what each level of the organization needs to know. One regulator of organizational information flow is the selective distribution of memoranda. Another mechanism is the selective use of training sessions.

Understanding the Agency's Mission

Training programs are clearly influenced by the nature of the agency (e.g., public or private), the characteristics of its clientele, the methods of operation, and the agency's stated goals. Each level of the organization views these factors somewhat differently, and different service units within the agency may have differing perceptions. In public welfare agencies, for example, support collection workers may view the agency as an agent of social control, protecting the taxpayer's dollars, while child protection workers may see the agency in terms of protecting the rights of children.

The mission of public human service agencies frequently reflects the same ambiguity that is found in social legislation. This ambiguity results, ultimately, from the competing values of promoting individual self-sufficiency and using public and private funds to serve those unable to help themselves. These same competing values affect the agencies' ability to enhance their workers' learning. From one perspective, the goal of training is to upgrade the workers' capacities to deliver services. On the other hand, limits that are placed on both the quantity and quality of services are also reflected in the content of training programs. The tension between efficiency and effectiveness of service delivery also affects the choices made in investing in staff training and development.

This duality of agency purpose makes it difficult to know what knowledge, skills, and attitudes should be paramount in a staff development program. For example, does the public agency want to enhance the effectiveness of staff in dealing with troubled clients or expand the skills of fraud investigators to reduce the incidence of welfare cheating? The decisions of agency administrators reflect the everyday answers to such questions and thereby the type of training that takes place. Training programs, as well as service programs in general, tend to reflect administrative values and interpretations of the agency's mission.

The organization's mission may be easier to identify by separating out three different types of goals:

1. goals related to client services;
2. internal operational goals related to the major job functions of staff required to maintain the operation of the organization; and
3. external survival goals related to enhancing the agency's position in the environment relative to competitors.

Agency personnel are generally more comfortable discussing service goals than organizational goals. Issues regarding competition for clients and program resources along with the issues of internal maintenance are difficult to articulate. In order not to appear self-serving, agencies often subvert management and survival goals. Service goals are reflected in the stated agency mission, and the time consuming management and survival goals are not formally recognized.

Agency staff development and training must address management and survival goals as well as service improvement goals. The stress of attempting to accomplish all three goals with declining resources can explain some of the confusion experienced by staff development specialists. Technical training often is perceived as serving the needs of the agency rather than client needs. Efforts directed toward maintaining the organization and improving its position in the community are as legitimate as focusing on the specific needs of clients.

The operational functions and tasks of top administrators will usually differ from those of line workers (e.g., presenting budgets vs. helping clients). However, these differences need to be accounted for in designing training programs so that each level of the organization is able to maintain a current understanding of others' domains. For example, presenting innovative treatment techniques to improve client services at a time when staff are preoccupied with reducing paperwork may be a recipe for failure. From the agency's perspective, training should enhance the mission of its programs, yet effective training must address the daily operational goals and objectives of workers as well.

Often, training programs are perceived as potential forums for clarifying the organizational mission goals. When this does occur, training activities become opportunities for organizational development that are usually designed to hold the organization together and move it toward particular goals. One of the requirements for productive organizational development processes is the involvement of top administrators, middle managers, and line workers. It is for this reason that trainers should exercise caution in mixing the training of line workers with the organizational development process of clarifying agency goals unless all key actors are involved.

Understanding Organizational Structure and Processes

In order to assess the role of staff development within an agency, it is necessary to understand the degree of centralization in the organization, the nature of the communication system, the existence of a reward system, and the role of the agency's external environment.

Centralization

The staff development manager must locate his or her position in the agency's organizational chart and identify the implications of such a position for managing a staff development program. Consider the three sections of different organization charts in figure 2.1 as alternative diagrams of administrative factors affecting training decisions. The critical factors suggested by the differences in the three models are (1) the degree to which the staff development function is centralized or decentralized and (2) its integration with other organizational functions. Section A is a decentralized model with both of the program divisions having their own training coordinator and presumably their own training programs. Section B is a centralized model located under administrative services, which usually includes such activities as personnel, accounting, and purchasing and may not be representative of the staff development needs of other program units. Section C is also a centralized model, with staff development located parallel to administrative services with equal access to the executive director. This option is most conducive to a comprehensive, agency-focused staff development program.

The advantage of the decentralized model is that staff development activities are more autonomous and training is easily tailored to meet the particular needs of each division. The advantage of the centralized model is the potential for more comprehensive pro-

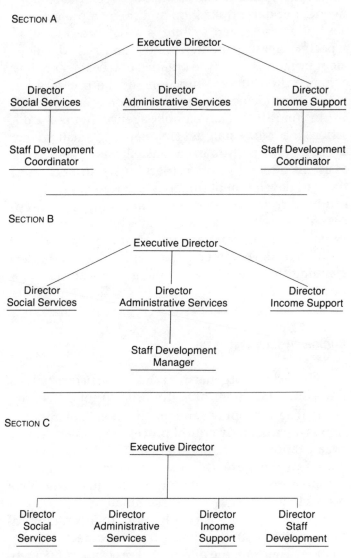

FIGURE 2.1.
*Alternative organizational locations of staff
development functions in large agencies.*

gram development. The balance between the responsiveness of decentralization and the comprehensiveness of a centralized system is a delicate one in all aspects of management. Training and staff development programs serve the organization best when they enhance the different functions of the organization without sacrificing the overall mission.

In contrast to a large public agency, figure 2.2 describes the role of staff development in a small private agency where part-time responsibility is located in the assistant director position (Section D). In Section E, the staff development function is delegated by the executive director to a staff committee composed of representatives from all levels in the organization. Whether public or private, the organizational location of the staff development function is critical in understanding the role and scope of agency staff development programs.

Communication Systems

The fact that organizations have a structure tells us that communications are supposed to follow certain paths. The appropriate and timely transfer of information is a particularly critical process in human service organizations where uncertain and complex environments are the norm. Information is a valued commodity and represents power for the individuals who have access to it and control its dissemination.

However, there is clearly more to a communications system than the simple transfer of factual information. There are the differential processes of perception, the managerial and political sifting and sorting and parcelling out of information, and the effects of so-

FIGURE 2.2.
Alternative organizational locations of staff development functions in small agencies.

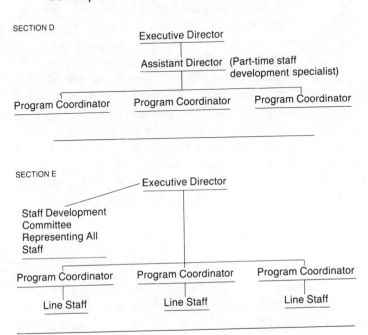

SECTION D

Executive Director

Assistant Director (Part-time staff development specialist)

Program Coordinator Program Coordinator Program Coordinator

SECTION E

Executive Director

Staff Development Committee Representing All Staff

Program Coordinator Program Coordinator Program Coordinator

Line Staff Line Staff Line Staff

cial interaction on individuals' ability to send and receive messages. The formal communication flow patterns are likely to correspond with the organizational chart. A "tall" hierarchy will likely have elaborate vertical (top-down) communications. A "flat" hierarchy is more characteristic of a decentralized agency and will display more horizontal communication. It is a well-documented but often ignored fact, however, that horizontal communications are the backbone of many social agencies regardless of formal structure.

Peer interactions and interunit communication keep the service delivery system moving.

The staff development manager should be aware of the formal and informal communication systems to detect communication problems that may affect or be affected by training. Training may be used to bridge such gaps. Needs assessments that result from surveying workers and supervisors must be interpreted in light of the vertical and horizontal and formal and informal communication patterns in the organization. Also important is an awareness of the political and human relations aspects of the organization, both as a staff development manager and as a competitor for internal resources. Isolation from agency politics may inhibit the development of a viable training program.

The Reward System

Another aspect of organizational analysis that is essential for the staff development manager is a review of the agency's reward system. Reward systems (with their implicit punishment options) are used to insure minimal standards and to motivate staff to improve job performance. While training should support these systems, it is not always a simple matter to identify how and what rewards are used. The reward system may vary from unit to unit within an agency.

Rewards are usually linked to compliance with job performance standards. Organizations achieve compliance with these standards in a number of ways. They may be categorized as coercive, remunerative, or normative (Etzioni, 1975). Only total institutions can be truly coercive in that residents are not free to leave. Coercion as a compliance strategy requires constant supervision and is therefore quite expensive. In human service agencies, as in other work organizations, it is assumed that staff perform adequately because they expect to be rewarded financially (remunerative) and/or because peer and community expectations encourage appropriate work-related behavior (normative). The staff development planning process, if it is to support efforts to achieve compliance with agency goals, must have clearly stated indicators of what constitutes adequate work performance. If such performance criteria are not available, the staff development manager should work with other managers to develop them.

Achieving compliance and adequate performance does not automatically translate into high quality service delivery. Motivation to do good work rather than just acceptable work is another management goal with direct implications for training. For example, it is widely held that remuneration (salary) as an expected reward is not very effective in motivating people to "go the extra mile" but serves to reduce dissatisfaction, similar to the role of supportive supervision and pleasant work conditions. Improving morale, therefore, does not necessarily result in improved service delivery. Motivation appears to be a function of the challenging nature of the work itself and how much potential it provides for achievement and recognition. *Training activities serve to enhance worker motivation when they increase the workers' prospects for developing new job-relevant abilities.*

Another aspect of the agency reward system is the nature of the personnel system, including civil service, unions, and professional certification. An important organizational goal is to relate the completion of training to career advancement within a personnel system.

Unfortunately, career ladders are usually not well delineated in human service organizations. The staff development specialist needs to be thoroughly familiar with the agency's personnel system in order to advocate career advancement opportunities and appropriate system changes. Needless to say, training that motivates workers to do excellent work will not always lead to worker advancement in the agency. The staff development specialist may be in the best administrative position to document such inconsistencies and seek changes from personnel managers and agency executives.

Understanding the Environment

The external environment of human service organizations requires constant attention in order to monitor pertinent news from the outside as it filters into the agency through different staff members. These persons act as organizational antennae interacting with other agencies, conducting research, and monitoring changes in the community. Keeping abreast of changes in the environment is a crucial activity for staff development specialists as well. Through training, the organization can better screen the complex, changing, and often conflicting information received from its environment.

Dill (1975:424) provides a framework for analyzing an organization's working environment in terms of: (1) customers, (2) suppliers, (3) competitors, and (4) regulatory groups. The customers or clients of a human service agency vary according to the different programs administered by the agency (e.g., an economically self-sufficient couple attempting to adopt a child, a mother on public assistance, or a developmentally disabled adult). The trainer must be aware of the breadth of problems that the agency's clientele present in order to assess the training needs of staff.

The agency's suppliers include the sources of labor, materials, equipment, capital, and physical space. Both public and many private agencies are dependent upon government for financial resources. Each agency program has its own funding formula for federal, state, and local contributions, thereby creating a complex network of interorganizational relationships. Additionally, some public agencies engage in considerable third-party contracting involving the purchase of services for a client from another source (e.g., large institutions, nursing homes, daycare centers for children, and a variety of specialized agencies). Training is being used increasingly to deal with the quality control issues inherent in such contracting.

Agencies compete with each other for financial resources and desirable clients. For selected clients, this competition is evident in the lack of cooperation in case management and program development efforts. Training programs often reflect the need to address these issues. Similarly, treatment fads can sweep through communities and foster competition among agencies seeking to promote the techniques of the latest expert.

For human service agencies, the regulatory function tends to be assumed by the federal or state agencies that also serve as suppliers. However, the enforcement of regulations usually emanates from a different set of offices in each agency than those that act as suppliers, thereby creating another system of environmental influences. A common complaint of public administrators and workers is that multiple sources of regulation produce incoherent and at times conflicting policies. Trainers need to be aware of how such conflicts can complicate training programs.

Another aspect of the agency's environment that directly affects staff development planning is the amount of change occurring. Political and policy shifts, the development of new knowledge, or budget demands may produce changes of clientele, equipment, forms, or procedures, or they may change the design and purpose of the service offered. The major sources of change for public agencies are the federal and state legislatures and agencies. The enactment of a new law, the repeal or revision of an existing law, and the promulgation of new policies and procedures by regulatory bodies account for most of the major changes. Dozens of administrative directives are received each month, the large majority of which prompt change somewhere in the agency.

Voluntary agencies, though less vulnerable to government-imposed change, must respond to changing demands for services as perceived by their boards. Regardless of the source of the changes, it is essential that the staff development manager be aware of their training implications. For example, if an agency board decides to develop new roles for volunteers as service providers, the staff development manager will want to address the volunteers' training needs as well as the staff's training needs regarding the appropriate deployment of volunteers.

This section has highlighted the important components of organizational structure and processes: centralization, communications, rewards, and the external environment. Analyzing an agency in terms of these components represents an important foundation for developing a staff development plan. In the next section, particular attention is given to balancing the staff development needs of the organization with those of the staff and the steps required for developing a plan.

Using Organizational Analysis for Staff Development Planning

How, then, does a manager address the question of who needs what knowledge, skills, and attitudes in an organization comprised of disparate, changing, and sometimes independent units? Based on the agency's mission, the staff development manager's role is to develop a training program that will motivate employees toward productive compliance with that mission as well as to ensure that the staff have the necessary knowledge and skills. As noted earlier, such compliance is achieved through some combination of remuneration and social reinforcement. While compliance is most likely to be enhanced by a staff development plan that recognizes both agency and worker perspectives, a negotiation process must take place in order to incorporate both perspectives into a staff development program. An agency's staff development planning process, as noted in figure 2.3, should produce a detailed statement of how the organization will guide its members' development. In addressing the tension between centralization and decentralization, it should reflect the organization's mission from the viewpoint of management and line staff. Such a format places the staff development manager in a negotiator role between the mission of the organization as in-

FIGURE 2.3.
*The process of negotiating training
program objectives.*

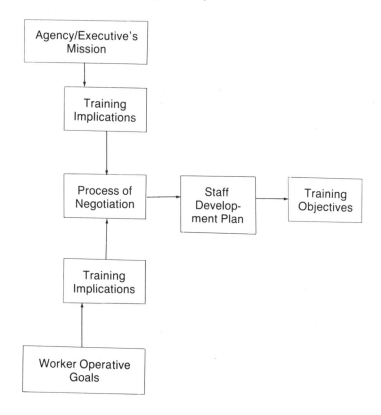

terpreted by the director and the perceived training
needs of line workers, who are implementing programs under complex and changing conditions. While
the two perspectives are not necessarily in conflict,
they are likely to be different. The training implications of each should be discernible from the staff de-

velopment manager's communication with appropriate staff and his or her own knowledge of the field. The negotiation process involves: (1) hearing the top administrator's interpretation of the agency's mission, its status in achieving that mission, and the current implications for training; (2) hearing line staff's interpretations of their operational goals and their training needs; and (3) assessing how other factors such as the agency's structure, internal processes, or its environment contribute to the similarity or dissimilarity between these two perspectives. The training objectives that emerge from the process can reflect the real and current training needs of the agency and serve as the foundation of a viable staff development plan.

Composition of the Staff Development Plan

One of the primary responsibilities of a staff development manager is the design of an agency staff development plan. A comprehensive staff development and training plan should include the following: (1) a statement of the purpose of staff development and training relative to the agency's mission; (2) a description of how training needs and priorities were assessed; (3) specification of training topics and resources to be used; (4) a rationale for each training component suggested; and (5) a description of how training programs will be implemented and evaluated.

In the *statement of purpose*, it should be made clear that all staff development and training efforts relate to the agency's mission by performing at least one of these three functions: orienting, updating, or upgrading staff. The plan should be clearly tied to the agency's goals and objectives, its new service directives, and its maintenance goals in a time of constricted resources. The linkage developed between staff training and organizational goals should be both realistic and explicit in the description of each training event.

The section on *how needs and priorities were assessed* includes both the process and results of the data-gathering phase of the planning process. The needs assessment component of staff development plans should reflect a systematic and creative approach for identifying high priority training needs in times of limited resources.

A description of the needs assessment process includes (1) the nature of the data gathering process; (2) the "formal" training needs assessment of workers; (3) a review of changes or anticipated changes in personnel or staffing patterns; and (4) a review of new policies and service directives that have training implications. The reporting of results of the needs assessment should be simple and direct in order to provide a clear rationale for each component of the training plan. Charts and graphs are particularly useful in reducing complex sets of figures into readable form. Information not directly related to the training plan will confuse and dilute the message. References to policy directives or regulations can be made concisely and effectively.

The *specification of training topics and resources* will vary in format with the size and complexity of the agency and its training function. Each planned training event should include a brief description of learning objectives, a *rationale for each component,* and details about trainers, time, and place. When there are a large number of training topics, list them in order of priority, with resources identified, as noted in figure 2.4.

A *description of how the training will be implemented* is an essential component of a well-designed plan. This section should include a description of the tasks to be accomplished and the responsibilities of all participants. The implementation method(s) should be justified in terms of: (1) how realistic, valid, and usable their results will be; (2) how feasible is implementation and evaluation; and (3) how the staff development manager will provide for overall monitoring of training and incorporation of results into the ongoing planning process. Included should be a justification of the agency's investment in training and staff development.

In summary, the components of an agency staff development plan are:

- Training needs (in order of priority)
- Description of training
- Trainee population (who and how many)
- Specific learning objectives
- Related agency objectives
- Projected training resources
- Estimated cost and duration of training
- Projected training dates

The description of these factors in the staff development plan will help relate the proposed training to the agency's ongoing planning processes.

Staff development planning is more than linking worker deficits and aspirations with available resources. The agency staff development plan is more than the simple sum of individual training needs or the total of each program's training needs. In order to

FIGURE 2.4.
Summary of staff development plan for Lakeside Child Care Center.

Training Needs (In order of priority)	Description of Training	Trainee Population (Who and how many)	Specific Learning Objectives	Related Agency Objectives	Projected Training Resources	Estimated Duration and Cost of Training	Projected Training Dates
Child development	Basic development stages	18 child care workers	To be able to identify behavior appropriate to development; to understand and be able to work with transition problems between stages	Providing therapeutic environment for emotionally disturbed children	School of Social Work faculty	6 hrs./$300	9/10/82
Orientation to community resources	Survey presentation of relevant community agencies, institutions, and probable natural helping networks	6 new child care workers and case workers	To be familiar with scope of various resources and how to access those resources	Strengthening families to promote successful return to home after residential treatment	Director and panel of community experts	3 hrs./no charge	10/12/82

Dealing with aggressive behavior	Alternative methods of behavior management with hostile children	18 child care workers	To reduce staff burnout through skill development; to increase social skills development of children in care	Providing therapeutic environment	Mental health consultant	6 hrs./$300	11/16/82
Staff supervision	Advanced skills in supervision	3 cottage supervisors	To improve leadership skills; to improve use of accountability systems	All objectives	Continuing education seminar, School of Social Work	2 days/$200	12/1-2/82

identify agency-wide issues appropriate for training, the staff development manager must engage in organizational analysis as part of the process of building a staff development plan. This analysis needs to take into account the agency's mission, its organizational structure and processes, and the impact of the agency's environment. Assessing the agency's functioning with regard to each of these issues will provide the staff development manager with the essential information needed for a staff development plan.

References

Dill, W. R. Environment as an Influence on Managerial Autonomy. *Administrative Science Quarterly,* 1975, 20, 613–629.

Etzioni, A. *A Comparative Analysis of Complex Organizations.* New York: Free Press, 1975.

March, J. G., and Simon, H. A. *Organizations.* New York: Wiley, 1958.

Chapter 3

How Does the Agency Take into Account the Worker's View of Staff Development Programs?

UP TO THIS POINT WE HAVE EMPHASIZED THE AGENCY PERspective on staff development, related primarily to analyzing social policies and organizational processes of agency life. Such top-down perspectives need to be balanced with the bottom-up views of direct service personnel. What is the worker's perspective of staff development? What motivates workers to advance their level of knowledge and skill? Do they seek self-improvement on the basis of improving their services to clients or in terms of individual definitions of professionalization? Do staff development workshops and training experiences serve as a source of new ideas to empower workers or simply as a reward for good behavior in the form of paid rest and relaxation? These difficult questions can be addressed through three major dimensions of the worker's view of staff development: (1) personal perspectives, (2) professional perspectives, and (3) organizational member perspectives. Empowering workers to recognize and utilize the benefits of staff development programs ought to be a primary goal of the staff development manager.

Personal Perspectives

For some human service workers, half-day to three-day staff development programs simply allow for some needed rest and relaxation (R&R) away from the office phone and work pressures. While rarely a stated training objective, this R&R approach could reflect the worker's frustration over agency communication problems, job stress, funding cutbacks, burnout, or skepticism about the value of brief training sessions. The R&R mentality may also reflect difficulties in shifting from job worries to a readiness to learn. In the minds of some workers, training sessions may be viewed as similar to the rote learning experiences of high school or college and therefore carry the old anti-learning or anti-intellectual baggage of years past.

For other human service workers, training experiences are viewed as opportunities to enhance one's practice by acquiring new knowledge and improving skills. Such workers display a readiness to learn that is often acquired from positive educational experiences in years past along with a receptiveness to learn from and interact with peers. They tend to view new learning opportunities in terms of increasing their job capacities and their professional skills. While their job and agency environment may be as stressful as that of others, these motivated workers actively engage in training experiences that they perceive as relevant to their careers. Others simply seek new knowledge out of a love of learning and a commitment to life-long learning. Such a positive orientation to training may also result from a supportive supervisor who actively seeks to connect training experiences to ongoing work demands.

While we have described two worker perspectives

on training, it should be clear that the two views represent extremes on a continuum since most workers reflect both the R&R and active learner orientation. For example, all workers can experience varying degrees of burnout irrespective of their orientation to learning. Therefore, it is important to identify multiple views of worker behavior, since human service agencies seek to address complex client problems, operate with inadequate resources to deal with the problems, and exist within societal expectations that are sometimes unrealistic or hostile to the goals of the agency. One view of how workers might perceive staff development programs can be gained from a study of public assistance caseworkers. Kroeger (1971) found four basic types of workers: (1) *advocates* who were positive toward the clients and negative towards the agency; (2) *bureaucrats* who were positive towards the agency and negative towards clients; (3) *apathetics* who were negative towards clients and the agency; and (4) *mediators* who were positive towards clients and the agency. If these types hold true for a variety of human service agencies, then it may be important to structure learning experiences in staff development programs in order to account for different types of workers.

Another perspective on how workers might view their organization and its staff development programs emerges from the research on burnout. Cherniss (1980) identified four different definitions of burnout: (1) occupational tedium reflected in physical, emotional, and attitudinal exhaustion; (2) loss of concern for the people with whom one is working; (3) psychological withdrawal from work in response to excessive stress or dissatisfaction including loss of enthusiasm, excitement, and a sense of mission about one's work; and (4) worker separation or withdrawal from the original meaning or purpose of one's work as reflected in estrangement from clients, co-workers, and the agency. Staff development managers need to understand burnout behaviors in terms of three distinct phases: (1) *stress,* which results from an imbalance between the worker's resources to do the job and the agency's demand to get the job done; (2) *strain,* which is a response to this imbalance and can be seen in the form of tension, anxiety, fatigue, and exhaustion; and (3) *defensive coping,* which is characterized by a detached and mechanical treatment of clients or a cynical preoccupation with gratifying one's own needs (Cherniss, 1980).

It is not clear how much responsibility the agency should assume for job-related burnout and how much the worker should assume. However, it is clear what most workers want. "What workers want most . . . is to become masters of their immediate environments and to feel that their work and they themselves are important—the twin ingredients of self-esteem. . . . An increasing number of workers want more autonomy in tackling their tasks, greater opportunity in increasing their skills, rewards that are directly connected to the intrinsic aspects of work, and greater participation in the design of work and the formulation of their tasks" (Cherniss, 1980: 154). Most workers seek relief from being overloaded with cases, oppressed by ineffective administrative rules and regulations, and apprehensive about job security and agency survival.

In the decades ahead we may see more and more workers taking responsibility for their own staff development needs. Some may pursue university continuing education workshops or certificate programs. Others may seek more personalized learning through the development of peer support groups, sometimes out of a sense of frustration that agency staff development programs are too basic, too narrowly focused, or too theoretical. There is a growing interest in using support groups as a means for enhancing job-related and personal growth and development. Kirschenbaum and Glaser (1978) define support groups as small groups of professionals with common areas of interest who meet periodically to learn together and support one another in maintaining ongoing professional development. The goals of most support groups include the exchange of new ideas, provision of practical help to group members, and the promotion of a sense of emotional support. Support groups may be formed within an agency, from among several agencies in a community, or from a variety of profit and nonprofit organizations. Agency trainers or staff development committees can facilitate the development of support groups inside and outside the agency by identifying common interests among staff and informing staff about the ways in which support groups can elicit new ideas, provide practical assistance, and promote a sense of support among their members.

Professional Perspectives

Professional perspectives, as distinguished from personal perspectives, relate both to the knowledge and skills that human service workers seek to expand and the capacities to assess one's career development needs in the context of life-long learning. The acquisition of new knowledge and skill is frequently viewed in the light of increasing one's chances of success in treating or serving clients. Such pursuits also provide staff with a sense of personal and professional fulfillment, enhancing one's professional self. Frequently the assessment of career development needs is carried out in terms of progressing from one job to another rather than within the context of the current job.

Most workers have a clear understanding of formal career progression related to exploring occupations, entering the first job, gaining promotion and seniority, acquiring a responsible position, and preparing for retirement. There is less clarity about one's informal career stages such as personal self-assessment and exploration, developing an occupational self-image as a worker, developing a self-concept as a co-worker and peer, managing success and failure, handling feelings of seniority or "having made it," acquiring a new sense of growth and maturity, and learning to accept the aging process and deceleration. Van Maanen and Schein (1977) have identified three stages of career socialization including entry, encounter, and transformation. The entry stage is often characterized as "stumbling into my career," followed by building expectations and justifications that rationalize the choice of occupation or profession. The shock of entry involves the encounter stage, in which disillusionment can result from job assignments that are too easy or too difficult. The shock is reduced by the supervisor's conscious use of a "honeymoon period" in which the worker adjusts, correctly and incorrectly, to the expectations of others in the agency. In this stage the peer group either reduces or amplifies the impact of the shock. Peer groups are usually quite supportive by helping the newcomer understand what constitutes a mistake within the group and the agency and by defending the newcomer's right to make a mistake.

The third and final stage, called transformation, involves the worker's resolution of the problems that emerged in the previous stage of encounter. Transformation includes the internalizing of agency norms and values and reflects the worker's increasing comfort and familiarity with the agency's environment. The worker develops a philosophical perspective on agency problems that is useful in negotiating a psychological contract with the supervisor in relationship to career interests, role expectations, group membership, and performance evaluations.

During the stages of entry, encounter, and transformation, career anchors emerge in the form of (1) managerial competence, (2) technical competence, (3) security, (4) creativity, and (5) autonomy and independence (Van Maanen and Schein, 1977). An anchor represents a combination of talents, values, and motives that have an impact on career decisions and usually contribute to one's sense of identity. Anchors usually emerge from the gradual discovery of what one is ''good at'' and what one values or likes to do. As Van Maanen and Schein (1977) have noted, if people move into settings in which they are likely to fail or in which their values are compromised, they will be pulled back into something more congruent with their skills and beliefs, hence the anchor metaphor.

The *managerial competence* anchor implies that workers seek and value opportunities to manage. If management activities serve as strong motivators, then the interpersonal competence, analytic competence, and emotional maturity to assume responsibilities and leadership will be decisive factors in gaining promotion to managerial positions. The *technical competence* anchor relates to exercising technical talents and areas of competence (e.g., the veteran teacher, nurse, or social worker who maintains a senior position with direct contact with pupils, patients, or clients). This anchor applies to workers who resist being promoted out of a technically satisfying role into a primarily managerial role. The *security* anchor dominates workers who are more concerned with job security than job challenge as they seek to stabilize their careers by subordinating their needs and desires to those of the agency (i.e., the organization man or woman). The *creativity* anchor includes the overarching need to build or create one's own product that is an extension of self, identified by name, and a measure of his or her accomplishments. The last anchor, *autonomy and independence,* relates to workers who seek work situations in which they are free from agency constraints to pursue their technical competence, where needs for autonomy exceed the need to exercise technical competence.

In addition to understanding the career development process, staff development managers and staff training committees need to address the degree to which training opportunities provide for enhanced professional knowledge and skills. One of the most difficult self-assessment processes for workers to conduct on their own is the monitoring and measuring of one's own professional growth. Without the stimulus of formal educational experiences or job-related requirements to document gaps in knowledge and skills, workers sometimes find it difficult to identify specific new knowledge and skills directly related to their work. The data for such self-assessments can be found in comprehensive job performance evaluations that include strengths and areas for improvement, new agency directives requiring new knowledge and skills (e.g., shift from serving middle-class outpatient clients to serving poor, chronically mentally ill patients in a day treatment program), and new service delivery techniques that require additional knowledge and skills.

Another important opportunity for self-assessment occurs when a worker has returned to the job from a training experience. In such situations supervisors need to encourage the testing and utilization of the new learning. One method that the supervisor might employ is helping workers plan one or more presentations to co-workers about the learning experience. This investment in planning by the supervisor and the worker probably represents, for example, less than 5 percent of the cost incurred by the agency in sending a worker away to a week-long workshop. And yet this small investment may prove to be the decisive factor in acquiring a benefit for the agency and in solidifying new learning by the worker.

Benne (1967: 300–301) identified several characteristics of the worker who has returned from a training experience, as follows:

1. *The easy convert.* Worker who has been passive in the learning environment, taking it all in with no struggle, and returns to the agency, puts on the "old shell," where no one notices any differences in behavior, knowledge, or attitude.
2. *The tourist.* Worker who approaches training as a visitor, inspecting what goes on, and returns to the agency with a package of techniques and papers, but no real change.
3. *The expatriate.* Worker who left agency with high

degree of anticipation and became deeply involved in the training experience, only to discover that the new ideas didn't have the same impact back in the agency.
4. *The missionary.* Worker who approached the training experience with a zeal for change and is over-eager in seeking to promote similar change back in the agency.
5. *The self-mystic.* Worker who underwent significant changes as result of training experience, but cannot explain what happened (e.g., ''It was a terrific experience''); often needs more time to sort things out.
6. *The learner-critic.* Worker who takes tough-minded, reality testing attitude toward learning experience, continuously compares new learning with agency realities, and is usually the most likely candidate for successfully transferring learning back into improved job performance.

Benne (1967) further defines the learner-critic as a person who stays marginal in order to account for the realities of both the training experience and the agency life, reflects a commitment to improving agency life but also studies and criticizes the agency, risks the negative reactions of co-workers, accepts the potency of new ideas, uses the supervisor as sounding board, honestly presents needs for agency changes by making new learning available to others, and accepts himself or herself as a person with more autonomy and spontaneous competence in problem solving and receiving feedback.

Obviously, staff learn in many different ways. Some learn by observing others, some learn by means of new or expanded job assignments, and still others learn by participating in formal and informal learning environments. Therefore the professional perspective can best be understood by the identification and documentation of worker learning styles. When training funds are scarce and the potential for staff burnout is high, it is critical for staff development managers to be in tune with the workers' perspectives on professional development.

Organizational Member Perspectives

Workers view their agencies from many different perspectives. In the area of training, they usually see more attention given to orienting and updating staff than to upgrading job performance through the acquisition of new knowledge and skills. Beyond orienting, updating, and upgrading staff, agency training can provide an opportunity for an individual to clarify his or her own job. In this section the perspectives of organizational members or workers are viewed through the lens of a job or job description.

Most human service jobs are poorly defined and rarely documented in current and comprehensive job descriptions. As a result, workers can spend an immense amount of time either guessing what their supervisors expect or interpreting their job in the context of past experiences, client needs, and old habits. Therefore, it is important to identify the essential elements of human service work, the standard processes for responding to client needs, and the approach to specifying the essential tasks of a job. These three components of job clarification are related to worker training experiences in the following ways: (1) the identification of training needs (noted in the next chapter) is directly related to the worker's understanding of his or her job; (2) the worker's readiness for using training opportunities is related to the clarity of the job description; and (3) the worker's receptivity to the actual training experiences is a function of his or her active use of job-related experiences in acquiring the new knowledge and skills presented. With these factors in mind, it's useful to highlight the nature of human service work and the role of worker tasks.

For the purpose of this discussion, social service work can be defined in terms of the following five major functions: (1) *linkage,* which includes brokering, referring, and advocating for clients; (2) *mobilization,* which includes developing resources and advocating for change in organizations and social policies; (3) *counseling,* which includes instructing, coaching, and supporting clients along with consultation to other care givers; (4) *treatment,* which includes maintaining and controlling the condition of clients through different therapies and care-giving activities; and (5) *administration,* which includes the collecting and processing of client information for service planning and evaluation. Social service staff can perform a number of different work roles which relate to each of these five functions. For example, brokering between the client and the resources of the community and advocating to protect the rights of clients represent two major work roles related to the linkage functions (Austin, 1979).

Case management is a good example of a job or job activities that include aspects of all five functions. Case management from the worker's and client's perspective involves the joint assessment of client needs and requests in terms of the client's capabilities to utilize the agency's services as well as the services of other community resources. Selected training implications for the following case management activities are noted in figure 3.1 (Boserup, 1977): (1) evaluating the need or request, (2) determining client eligibility, (3) planning for the provision and/or arrangement of services, (4) arranging for the delivery of services, (5) providing services, (6) overseeing service delivery, and (7) recording progress toward service goals. Figure 3.1 illustrates how work can be analyzed for its staff development implications by raising questions about the nature and quality of service. These same questions can be used as part of a job performance evaluation.

In addition to an understanding of case management activities, it is important to add the more specific worker tasks to our overall conceptualization of social service work. While traditional job descriptions rarely reflect the full breadth and depth of the work performed, it is possible to understand social service work by analyzing the tasks performed by workers. The task analysis process involves a complete assessment of the range of actions or action sequences that workers perform in meeting the service objectives developed in collaboration with clients (Austin, 1981). An example of a task profile for a worker in a youth corrections agency is noted in figure 3.2. Such a task profile gives detailed information about what the worker actually does, describes a large segment of work to be completed in line with agency expectations, and provides a foundation for identifying components of the job that need more staff development attention for one or more workers. Such a description should result from a mutual sharing process between the worker and the agency's management representative, the supervisor.

FIGURE 3.1.
Case management or managing cases:
Training implications for agency personnel.

I. EVALUATING THE CLIENT NEED OR REQUEST

   1. Does the written documentation of client need or request reflect observable, tangible evidence that is within the purview of the agency's responsibility?

   2. Did the client experience any difficulty in gaining access to the agency?

   3. Is the judgment about the screening "in" or screening "out" of the prospective client fully documented and justified?

II. DETERMINING CLIENT ELIGIBILITY

   1. Is all pertinent information noted on client intake form?

   2. Are clients advised of their rights and responsibilities? How is this documented?

   3. Is client eligibility determined by a careful matching of client need with the agency's service criteria and priorities?

III. PLANNING FOR THE PROVISION AND/OR ARRANGEMENT OF SERVICES

   1. To what extent is the client assisted in identifying the presenting problems and uncovering relevant facts?

   2. To what extent is the client involved in the establishment of service objectives?

   3. To what extent are the client and other service providers and support networks involved in identifying relevant service programs?

   4. To what extent does the service plan reflect estimated times for reaching service objectives and periodic reporting activities related to client progress?

   5. To what extent does the service plan account for short-term and long-term objectives and aspects of the problems that clients can be expected to handle on their own?

IV. ARRANGING FOR THE DELIVERY OF SERVICES

   1. Are the planning and arranging activities fully documented in the client's records?

   2. Are all relevant service providers listed with information about client follow-up activities?

   3. Are inter-agency and intra-agency communication processes monitored regularly and modified if necessary?

FIGURE 3.1. (*continued*).

V. PROVIDING SERVICES

    1. Are specific counseling or treatment services provided on a regular basis to the client with the monitoring of progress noted in the client's record?

    2. Are specific support services (e.g., homemaker, meals on wheels, day care, etc.) provided on a regular basis to the client and monitored by other services providers?

VI. MONITORING SERVICE DELIVERY

    1. Was the client situation accurately noted upon entry into the agency?

    2. What services have been received?

    3. What conditions have changed since the service plan was developed?

    4. Is progress being made toward service objectives?

    5. Should the service plan be changed?

    6. Should the case be closed?

VII. RECORDING PROGRESS TOWARD SERVICE GOALS

    1. Is information recorded in the case record pertinent to each of the preceding activities?

    2. Are case records purged of outdated material?

    3. Is the recording process structured in an efficient manner in order not to dominate the case management process?

It requires periodic updating if it is to be a workable and useful contract that captures both the worker's and the agency's perspectives.

In summary, the worker's perspective of the agency's investment in staff development relates to both personal and organizational change. The personal change is linked to the agency's understanding of career planning and the personal attributes of worker growth and burnout. The organizational change involves the agency's recognition that organizational life can be improved through a variety of staff development and organizational development strategies.

FIGURE 3.2.

Sample task profile for a direct service worker in a youth corrections agency.

I. EVALUATING THE CLIENT NEED AND DETERMINING ELIGIBILITY

1. Discusses problem situation (emotional, medical, administrative, etc.) with present or potential service client, during office visit or conversation (phone or casual), using knowledge of service resources, advising clients of availability of resources in order to refer same to appropriate resource.
2. Talks with client (or relation), exploring problems, answering questions when necessary, in order to calm same (allay fears, release anxiety, reassure, support).
3. Questions (interviews) client regarding status of particular aspect of case (school attendance, employment, transportation, address, etc.), using telephone or personal visit in order to determine current need or status, or to update case information.
4. Interviews client, gathering background information, in order to compile social history.
5. Screens case file(s) or client records relative to specific information, in order to determine individual status or compile list of clients with certain characteristics.

II. PLANNING FOR THE PROVISION OF SERVICES

6. Informs client of the results of medically related tests or problems explaining implications in order to discuss (explore) indicated follow-up.
7. Discusses aspect of administration of treatment (or treatment plan or program) with client (and/or relation), informing, clarifying, briefing, debriefing, or answering questions in order to promote understanding (or to allay fears).
8. Explains rules (or program or agreement) to client(s), answering questions when asked, in order to orient (or reorient) same to a particular program.
9. Discusses case with relation of client, collecting specific information, in order to monitor case status for case planning purposes.
10. Collects client specific information from service system colleague in order to receive information necessary for service planning (monitoring, verifying, or service provision).

FIGURE 3.2. (*continued*).

11. Discusses client situation with service system colleague in order to exchange information useful in service planning or service provision.
12. Reports client specific information (orally or in writing) to service system colleague (judges included) in order to provide information for service planning (or service provision or case action).

III. ARRANGING FOR THE DELIVERY OF SERVICES

13. Discusses case situation with service representative (initiating the linkage of a client with an appropriate resource) in order to arrange an appointment for services.
14. Transports client to specific destination(s) using public or private vehicle in order to link client with service or treatment resource.
15. Confers with colleagues in staffing (team, court unit, or committee) meeting, providing and/or receiving information as required for understanding, in order to reach decision regarding disposition of specific cases.
16. Discusses case situation with relative, using personal visit, written correspondence, or telephone, planning alternate care for client (foster home, return to home, home visit, respite care, hospitalization, etc.), in order to arrange suitable or appropriate environment.
17. Confers with service system colleague(s) on specific case(s), or specific client group, corresponding when appropriate, reaching mutual agreement on details of service (case actions) and individual responsibilities in order to coordinate or implement services.
18. Authorizes services by issuing ID cards, signing off, writing orders, etc., using personal authority according to standard operating procedures (SOP), in order to effect the receipt of particular services or treatment to a client.

IV. PROVIDING SERVICES

19. Counsels with client(s) or relative, preventing undesirable behavior when necessary, in order to motivate same toward acceptable (responsible) behavior.
20. Counsels client (and/or members of family), using recognized intervention methods and operational knowledge of particular agencies, advising same of consequences when appropriate, in order to improve social functioning and/or to reconcile relations.

FIGURE 3.2. (*continued*).

V.   MONITORING SERVICE DELIVERY

21. Investigates breach of service plan (for aberrant behavior or complaint), discussing situation with client's relations or collaterals, in order to determine facts.
22. Reviews case with client, evaluating present status (or progress), discussing situation when appropriate, in order to recommend continued or appropriate treatment.
23. Reviews case records (or client reports or information), evaluating information in order to develop or change treatment plans.
24. Discusses administrative matters with colleague(s), reviewing relevant issues, operating procedures, policies, administrative problems, etc., with them, reporting relevant information, clarifying issues, in order to inform, coordinate, plan, or decide.

VI.   RECORDING PROGRESS TOWARD SERVICE GOALS

25. Drafts (dictates) client reports (progress, discipline, incident), using case records and knowledge of case situation, recommending plans when indicated, in order to compile written information for service planning.
26. Records personal travel, using standard reporting form, in order to summarize items for reimbursement.

From a worker's perspective, staff development programs can help to solidify one's identity in the agency, as a valued member of an organizational family. Such programs can help increase loyalty to the agency as well as enhance the development of the work group or service unit. Being valued by the agency in terms of being granted released time for staff development programs can increase and/or reaffirm a worker's commitment to delivering high quality services and to contributing to a positive work environment. Enlightened administrators recognize these benefits and thereby seek to provide staff develop-

ment programs to enhance worker growth and development. In such cases, workers have come to expect
the availability of training programs as part of their
rights as agency employees.

We began this chapter with a series of questions
related to the worker's perspective on staff development. Since worker motivation to seek self-
improvement is complicated by differences in personalities, work experience, agency environments, home
environments, and basic values, we selected the following three dimensions of a worker's perspective on
staff development as a means for untangling this complex web of forces: (1) the personal perspective, (2) the
professional perspective, and (3) the organizational
member perspective.

While the worker's perceptions of the agency may
not match those of a staff development manager, it is
crucial that worker perceptions be understood as real
and therefore significant factors influencing a worker's view of staff development. The worker perspective can be understood in relationship to the need for
staff growth and peer support, for counteracting the
effects of burnout, and for career development. In so
doing, the staff development manager or staff development committee can continuously assess the interaction between the operation of the agency and the
worker's progression through career stages. This interaction will influence the planning, implementation,
and outcome of staff development programming. The
interaction can also be a focal point for analyzing staff
growth as well as burnout.

Understanding the nature of social service functions and job tasks is an important foundation for
building staff development programs. Without this
foundation workers will experience considerable frus-

tration in their efforts to link training content to their everyday job content. The goal of this chapter was to highlight the important aspects of the worker's perspective on staff development. These issues, unfortunately, are frequently overlooked in the staff development planning and implementation process.

References

Austin, M. J. Designing Human Services Training Based on Worker Task Analysis. In Clark, F. W., and Arkava, M. L. (Eds.), *The Pursuit of Competence in Social Work*. San Francisco, Calif.: Jossey-Bass, 1979.

Austin, M. J. *Supervisory Management for the Human Services*. Englewood Cliffs, N.J.: Prentice-Hall, 1981.

Benne, K. D. The Transfer of Learning: Six Models for Man in Transition. In Lynton, R. P., and Pareek, V. (Eds.), *Training for Development*. Homewood, Ill.: Richard D. Irwin, 1967.

Boserup, D. G. *The Case Management Model*. Athens, Ga.: Regional Institute for Social Welfare Research, 1977.

Cherniss, C. *Staff Burnout: Job Stress in the Human Services*. Beverly Hills, Calif.: Sage Pubns, 1980.

Kirschenbaum, H., and Glaser, B. *Developing Support Groups: A Manual for Facilitators and Participants*. La Jolla, Calif.: University Associates, 1978.

Kroeger, N. Organizational Goals, Policies, and Output. The Dilemma of Public Aid. Unpublished doctoral dissertation, University of Chicago, 1971.

Special Task Force to the Secretary of Health, Education, and Welfare. *Work in America*. Cambridge, Mass.: MIT Press, 1973, p. 13.

Van Maanen, J., and Schein, E. H. Career Development. In Hachman, J. R., and Suttle, J. L. (Eds.), *Improving Life at Work: Behavioral Science Approaches to Organizational Change*. Santa Monica, Calif.: Goodyear Pub., 1977.

Chapter 4

How Can Trainers Measure and Document the Training Needs of Staff?

ENHANCING THE KNOWLEDGE AND SKILLS OF ALL STAFF IS the central mission of a staff development program. As such, staff development programs can significantly affect staff and organizational performance by serving as a "bridge between the qualities and resources of available personnel and the needs and styles of diverse client populations" (Maluccio, 1977:8). Staff development is any process or program to improve staff performance by enhancing work-relevant knowledge and skills. Planned instruction, reading, experiential learning, and other methods are used to increase worker effectiveness (Clegg, 1966; Fine, 1979).

Additional staff development objectives include: (1) orienting new employees; (2) identifying worker performance deficiencies; (3) coping with legal, societal, economic, and technological changes so that the organizations can flexibly meet emerging needs and unexpected contingencies; (4) preparing and upgrading employees for more skilled positions and possible advancements; and (5) enabling employees to keep up with current developments in their field of specialization (Leonard, 1974:40). The central function of staff development, however, is to equip staff with the knowledge, skills, and attitudes necessary for effective job performance. This requires defining the specific need for training. A training need, therefore, refers to the gap between what "workers ought to know and be able to do in order to perform optimally in their jobs, and what they actually know and are proficient at doing" (Green, Dickinson, and Bremseth, 1979:8).

Assessing worker training needs is part of staff development planning and includes the specification of organizational goals and objectives, as well as essential job tasks and staff competencies (Zober, 1980). This chapter concentrates on the principles and practices of conducting a training needs assessment for planning staff development programs.

Importance of Training Needs Assessments

Training needs assessment involves (1) applying measurement tools to assess staff competence or performance, (2) analyzing the gathered information to determine training program goals and priorities, and (3) using the training program priorities to determine training objectives, curriculum activities, and evaluation (Schinke and Schilling, 1980; Warheit, Bell, and Schwab, 1977). With the increasing lack of agency resources for staff development programs, social service agencies are struggling to design more targeted training programs based on specific worker training needs. For example, a state social services department recently developed a foster care training program for their child welfare staff based only on the perceptions of administrators and supervisors. After receiving negative evaluations of a two-day training program, the state implemented a training needs assessment that indicated that staff needed more skills in writing goal-oriented case plans and in promoting the involvement of foster parents. With this new information, training sessions were reduced to one-day intensive workshops, and staff satisfaction with training and staff performance subsequently increased.

Given the importance of needs assessment, a wide range of methods exist for identifying staff training needs. State public welfare agencies commonly use a form of "information buildup" where training preferences of line staff are informally passed up the organizational ladder to top management and staff development personnel (Arkava, 1979). Information loss and distortion are minimized, however, when agencies use more structured needs assessment methods. This section will briefly outline methods for improving staff development needs assessment data through organizational performance analyses, critical incident methods, and objective or proficiency tests. The next section will address the techniques for generating more specific training needs assessment data from workers.

One method of assessing staff training needs is the documentation of organizational performance problems that can be addressed through specific training. While focusing on the "results" of job activities as reflected in program evaluations and organizational assessments, it is possible to identify issues that can be addressed through training and those that require administrative decision making related to organizational change. For example, poor case planning or management, a failure to specify or meet case goals, inappropriate referrals, and nonattainment of performance standards may all constitute marginal organizational performance, leading to both the specification of training needs and the need for organizational change (Johnson, 1967). The essential task of organizational analysis is to distinguish staff performance problems due to insufficient knowledge or skill from organizational problems due to system deficiencies. Sometimes the organizational analysis method is called an "organizational audit" that involves scrutinizing work activities, service delivery inputs and outputs, case records and reports, and worker efficiency and effectiveness. Service delivery systems and procedures are analyzed to identify deficiencies and make recommendations for specific improvements. Some of the organizational audit information is used for planning staff development programs (Morrison, 1976).

The Local Child Welfare Agency Self-Assessment Checklist is a good example of an instrument that could aid public social service agencies in their use of the organizational performance analysis approach (Sundel, Homan, Lucas, Burt, and Clarren, 1979). The checklist contains twenty major service goals that represent the major service delivery areas for child welfare agencies (e.g., provision of appropriate emergency services, conducting systematic intake investigations). Each goal is followed by a set of performance indicators that ask whether or not an agency's program is currently meeting that objective (e.g., In more than 10 percent of cases served within the past year, has further child abuse taken place after the delivery of some form of protective service?) The Self-Assessment Checklist has been used in several states as a way of identifying agency performance problems that might be addressed by staff training (Washington, Rindfleisch, Toomey, Bushnell, and Pecora, 1979). It is important to note, however, that a "translation process" is required to determine which of the organizational performance problems could be addressed through staff training as distinct from those requiring organizational change. This is less of a problem when more staff performance-oriented outcome measures are used (Magura and Moses, 1980).

In contrast to organizational analysis, a needs assessment could also be derived from "what ought to be" with emphasis placed on the "best social service practice" as determined by using the critical incident method. This method focuses on effective and ineffective practice behaviors and is a form of performance appraisal that can be used to identify training needs. Critical incidents are situations or events which reflect specific behaviors that have been found to make the difference between success and failure in delivering client services. For example, frontline staff and supervisors could rate the event or "critical incidents" in which their possession of knowledge or skill made the difference between success or failure (e.g., establishing a time and goal-oriented case plan for serving a child entering foster care). The *truly critical* incidents can be categorized into organizational performance areas and used for training needs assessment. For example, when a significant number of staff in a particular program or unit identify critical incidents related to the ineffective delivery of services, the staff development specialist can use the needs assessment information for designing training events to help improve work behavior patterns in that organizational unit (Maveske, Harmon, and Glickman, 1966; Morrison, 1976).

While organizational analysis is a useful approach

to developing needs assessment data, there are more specific worker-based techniques, and the remainder of this chapter will address four of them: the nominal group technique, key informant or allied professional interviews, knowledge-based surveys, and worker ability/characteristic surveys.[1] Each technique will be described in terms of format, data analysis and use, strengths and limitations, and general issues relating to instrument selection and training priorities.

The Nominal Group Technique

Definition

The nominal group technique involves a structured group meeting which can be used to identify staff training needs (Delbecq, Van de Ven, and Gustafson, 1975; Rindfleisch, Toomey, and Soldano, 1979). In one sense, it constitutes the documentation of a verbal discussion among agency personnel who may have gathered together in small groups. The nominal group technique can be used for individual brainstorming and small group discussion of worker training needs, agency performance problems, and possible training formats. Using the nominal group technique to identify staff training needs involves the following steps:

1. *Group Member Identification and Convocation.* Workers, supervisors and other individuals who are considered knowledgeable about staff training needs

are gathered together in groups of five to nine members.

2. *Silent Generation of Ideas in Writing.* The group discussion leader reads an open-ended statement or asks the question of interest (e.g., The five most important training needs of the outreach staff are _____?). Group members are then asked to work alone for about five minutes writing down their ideas or recommendations.

3. *Round-Robin Recording of Ideas on a Flip Chart.* This step involves recording the ideas of group members on a flip chart or blackboard visible to the entire group. Round-robin recording means going around the table and asking for one idea from one member at a time. The group leader writes the idea or recommendation of a group member in a short phrase on the flip chart and then proceeds to ask for one idea from the next group member in turn. The process is repeated until the ideas of every group member are listed. The group leader should record each idea or recommendation in the member's own words, condensing it only with the help of the respondent. In addition, if a group member has exhausted his or her list of five ideas but thinks of another idea based on the ideas of others, he or she should be encouraged to add it to the group's list.

4. *Serial Discussion for Clarification.* The next step of the nominal group process involves clarifying and briefly discussing each item. Starting with the first idea, members should now be allowed to clarify or speak freely about the importance of each item. During this process, the group (with the consent of contributors) may decide to add words to clarify an item. The central object of the discussion is to clar-

ify items, not to win arguments. The leader should avoid lengthy discussions on any one particular item.

5. *Voting on Item Importance.* Group members are asked to select five topic areas that they perceive to be most important. Members are then asked to vote, and the votes are recorded next to each item on the flip chart or blackboard. When the top five or more ideas are determined, participants are asked to rank the items according to their perception of each item's importance.[2]

Data Analysis and Use

To prepare a final list of training needs or subject areas selected by group members, mark the items with the highest number of votes. The item with the highest score is the most important training need or subject area. The rest of the items should be listed in descending order. This listing can now be used in conjunction with other needs assessment data or used by itself to plan training.

Strengths

A significant number of social service agencies are small in size and are not able to plan or conduct extensive needs assessment studies. The nominal group technique is especially useful for these agencies and for decision making by staff development committees.

In particular, one strength of this technique is that it involves two major needs assessment subactivities:

fact-finding (problem search and generation of ideas) and evaluation (information synthesis, screening, and choice of alternatives). A second strength is the attention given to each idea or recommendation and the opportunity for each individual to ensure that his or her ideas are part of the group's frame of reference (Delbecq et al., 1975). A third strength is the use of ranking or rating procedures where the addition of simple numbered voting procedures can greatly reduce errors in aggregating individual judgments into group decisions (Huber and Delbecq, 1972). Finally, when used for assessing training needs, the nominal group technique generates many unique ideas and is among the most straightforward and inexpensive method available.

Limitations

One issue that may be problematic with the nominal group technique is the representativeness or degree of job familiarity of the members who comprise the group. Because this technique uses small groups, members should be carefully chosen for their representativeness or familiarity with the actual training needs of staff. There is also a potential for significant bias if some group members have more organizational authority or power than other members. However, if the steps and procedures are skillfully used, this biasing effect can be minimized. Finally, this needs assessment technique relies heavily on the degree of group members' understanding of the issue or question under discussion and their ability to interpret job functions in order to identify important staff training needs.

The Key Informant or Allied Professional Interview Method

Definition

The key informant approach to identifying worker training needs involves soliciting information about organizational problems and staff training needs from persons outside the agency who have knowledge about staff performance. For example, key informants for a child welfare agency might be consulting psychologists and psychiatrists, juvenile court judges and lawyers, mental health and school personnel, personnel in contract agencies, and foster parents. Because of the "spy" connotation of the term "key informant," the term "allied professional" is used.

Allied professionals can be selected from a list of names recommended by agency administrators, from a random sample of persons recommended by a staff development planning group, or by a peer nomination process whereby an agency executive identifies approximately six persons who in turn nominate five or more additional knowledgeable persons. After compiling a list of nominees, selections can be made based on the names of those with multiple nominations (Rindfleisch et al., 1979).

Data collection is usually accomplished through in-person or phone interviews, which provide an opportunity to use open-ended and probing questions to secure a wide range of information. Questions can focus on program strengths and limitations, difficult worker tasks, worker training needs, worker strengths, and preferred training methods.[3] Figure 4.1

FIGURE 4.1.
Example of an allied professional interview schedule.

INTERVIEWER _____
INTERVIEWEE _____
DATE/DURATION _____

The purpose of this interview is to obtain your observations of the kinds of training that could enhance the delivery of child and family social services by the state child welfare staff.

1. In what ways do you interact with the staff or clients of the Division of Family and Youth Services?
2. What staff responsibilities or activities do you think are the most difficult?
   For example?
3. What are some of the problems in the way that child and family services are presently delivered?
   Internal (I), External (E); For example?
4. Which problems could be addressed by training?
   For example?
5. What specific training would be necessary?
   For example?
6. In your opinion, in what areas are the staff the *least* prepared?
   For example?
7. What type of training activities would enhance job performance in the areas in which staff are least prepared?
8. What would be the most effective format for providing this training?
   In-house workshops ___   Conferences ___
   Academic coursework ___   Personal supervision ___
   Why? _____
9. In your opinion, in what areas are the staff the *best* prepared?
   For example?
10. What type of training activities would build upon these strengths?
    For example?

is an example of an allied professional survey that was used as an interview guide for a needs assessment study of child welfare staff (Pecora, 1982b). This survey could be sent in advance to allied professionals as a way of stimulating their thinking before the interview.

Data Analysis and Use

The open-ended questions on the allied professional survey can be analyzed by examining all the responses to each question, organizing them into categories or themes, and recording the intensity and frequency with which they were expressed. The information about service delivery problems, worker strengths, and staff training needs can be summarized in a descriptive report. Allied professional data is typically used to supplement and enrich other types of needs assessment data gathered through worker and supervisor surveys.

Strengths

The allied professional method is simple and inexpensive and can provide a large amount of information about worker training needs from sources outside the agency. It is a useful device for distinguishing service delivery problems from specific staff training needs. Consequently, allied professional data are often used by agencies to modify service delivery policies, programs, or procedures. In addition, it highlights program and worker strengths. Training can then be designed to build upon worker strengths as well as to correct worker deficiencies. Thus, the public relations aspects of interviewing allied professionals and community leaders and the identification of program and worker strengths are two important fringe benefits of this needs assessment method.

Limitations

A primary limitation of the allied professional method is its built-in bias because of the respondent's individual or organizational perspective. It has been demonstrated that allied professional or key informant data is most accurate if the respondents are chosen for their expertise in a particular area and then questioned only in reference to that area (Warheit, Buhl, and Bell, 1978).

Knowledge-based Method

Definition

This approach to training needs assessment is based on worker self-reports and uses a list of knowledge areas that are considered necessary for job performance. Using job analysis data, worker and supervisory committees, and/or social service consultants, a set of core knowledge or subject areas is compiled for use in a survey questionnaire. In completing the survey, workers indicate whether they want training to be provided in a subject area and, if so, the importance of training in that particular area for improving their job performance. The high priority subject areas can then be used in the development of a training program (Kirkpatrick, 1977).

In using a knowledge-based needs assessment survey it is assumed that agency staff are able to delineate the knowledge areas essential for adequate job performance. While this questionnaire method can quickly identify staff training preferences, it is occasionally supplemented by personal interviews with staff. An example of a knowledge-based questionnaire is noted in figure 4.2. This instrument can be easily adapted for use in a variety of social service programs by modifying the knowledge areas and some demographic items, noted in Section A on personal data and Section B on training conditions.[4]

To complete the knowledge area section of the survey (Section C), staff are requested to place a checkmark to the right of the knowledge areas for which they want training (column 1). For each knowledge area checked as a training need, respondents rate the importance of training for improving their job performance according to a four-point scale: (1) not so important, (2) fairly important, (3) important, and (4) crucial to improving my job performance. Two survey columns are included so that staff can review the list to select their training "needs." After reviewing the total list, staff then rate the importance of each area checked. Because staff review the total list first, they may weigh the importance of a particular item in relation to other training needs.

Noncomputer Data Analysis and Use

The worker characteristics and training conditions sections data should be analyzed by tabulating the re-

FIGURE 4.2.
An example of a knowledge-based needs assessment survey.

SECTION A: *Worker Characteristics*

YOUR AGENCY _____

PERSONAL INFORMATION: *Please check the most appropriate response.*

AGE:

1. ____ 19–25   ____ 26–30   ____ 31–35   ____ 36–40
   ____ 41–45   ____ over 45

EDUCATIONAL BACKGROUND: *Check only the highest level received.*

2. ____ less than high school   ____ high school graduate
   ____ some college   ____ Bachelor (Social Work)
   ____ Master (Social Work)   ____ BS/BA (other) _____
   ____ MS/MA (other) _____   ____ Ph.D. (other) _____
   ____ other _____
            (please specify)

WORK EXPERIENCE:

3. What is your current position title? (*Include level I, II, etc., if applicable*) _____

4. How many years have you been in your current position?

   ____ years   ____ months

5. About what percentage of your time do you spend doing each of the following functions as a part of your current position: (fill in as many as appropriate; total = 100%).

   ____ % emergency/protective   ____ % intake/service
   ____ % in-home services   choice
   ____ % adoption services   ____ % foster care
   ____ % residential group   ____ % other _____
           care   *(please specify)*

6. Of the above, which do you consider your *primary* area of service? _____

CLIENT CHARACTERISTICS:

The following questions describe clients on three different dimensions. In each question describe the population you serve.

FIGURE 4.2. (*Section A—continued*).

7. What percentage of your time do you spend serving the clients in these geographic areas? (total = 100%)

  ____ % urban
  ____ % rural
  ____ % other _____
  _____(please specify)_

8. Children's services staff work directly with children or on their behalf with adults in their lives. Of all children you serve, what percentage of your time do you spend working with or for the following age groups? (total = 100%)

  ____ % infant (0–2)   ____ % preschool (3–5)
  ____ % latency aged (6–10)   ____ % adolescents (11–18)
  ____ % adults

9. What percentage of your time do you spend serving people in each of these ethnic/cultural categories? (total need not equal 100%)

  ____ % Asian   ____ % Black
  ____ % Hispanic   ____ % Native American
  ____ % White   ____ % other _____
                         (please specify)

OPINIONS:

10. What do you feel are the advantages for *you* in taking training/education? (check all that apply)

  ____ get promoted
  ____ improve skill or knowledge
  ____ feel more competent to help clients
  ____ professional growth
  ____ prevent burnout
  ____ communicate with other professionals
  ____ keep up to date
  ____ personal growth
  ____ escape, travel
  ____ other _____
        (please specify)

The following statements measure your opinions about training. Circle the response which reflects your level of agreement.

(SA—Strongly Agree, A—Agree, N—Neutral, D—Disagree, SD—Strongly Disagree)

FIGURE 4.2. (*Section A—continued*).

11. My supervisor encourages me to take
    training/education courses. SA A N D SD

12. My agency supports workers' interests
    in additional training. SA A N D SD

13. I feel taking additional training is
    rewarded by my agency. SA A N D SD

14. I feel I need training in order to get a
    promotion or a raise. SA A N D SD

15. I feel current levels of training are
    adequate. SA A N D SD

SECTION B: *Conditions of Training*

Items on this questionnaire are designed to assess conditions
which support planning and utilization of training programs.

CONDITIONS FOR TRAINING:

Please indicate your preferences for obtaining education/training
for your *current* position.

1. What are the incentives that you are aware of that are
   offered by your employer to encourage you to further your
   education/training related to your current job?*(check all that
   apply)*
   ____ tuition reimbursement
   ____ released time/administrative leave
   ____ full time education leave
   ____ frequent
   ____ none
   ____ other _____
        (please specify)

2. Would you pursue additional education in a degree or
   certificate program if a fee-reimbursement were available
   through your agency?
   ____ yes   ____ no   ____ undecided

3. Would you pursue additional education in a degree or
   certificate program if educational leaves were available
   through your agency?
   ____ yes   ____ no   ____ undecided

FIGURE 4.2. (*Section B—continued*).

4. I prefer that the training is presented: (*check one*)

___ at my agency
___ at an outside facility in town
___ at an outside facility out of town
___ other _____
      (please specify)

5. I prefer that the training/education program is presented by: (Rank two. Indicate most preferred with a 1 and next preferred with a 2.)

___ agency staff   ___ state staff
___ outside consultants   ___ college/university staff
___ technical school staff   ___ other _____
                                                     (please specify)

6. I prefer the following time for training: (*check one*)

___ Monday–Friday (daytimes)
___ Monday–Friday (evenings)
___ Saturday

7. I would attend training scheduled on Saturdays.

___ yes   ___ no   ___ undecided

8. I would attend training scheduled on evenings.

___ yes   ___ no   ___ undecided

9. I would attend training that necessitated my being away from home overnight.

___ yes   ___ no   ___ undecided

10. I prefer the following types of training programs: (choose *three*—indicate the one you prefer *most* with a 1, the next best with a 2, and your third choice with a 3).

___ on the job
___ 1–2 day workshops
___ short sessions offered over a period of weeks
___ intensive 1 to 2 week programs
___ part time degree programs
___ courses at a vocation program
___ courses at a college/university
___ other _____
      (please specify)

11. Possible Barriers to Training: Check *all* that are appropriate and add any others you can identify.

___ I need child care on weekends or evenings.

FIGURE 4.2. (*Section B—continued*).

____ I can't stay away from home overnight.
____ I do not have enough time.
____ No chance for promotion.
____ The courses I want are not available.
____ My agency will not give me release time.
____ My agency will not pay for training.
____ I don't know where to apply for appropriate training.
____ other _____
       (please specify)

SECTION C: *Knowledge Area Training Needs*

SCALE OF IMPORTANCE
1. Not so important
2. Fairly important
3. Important
4. Crucial to improving
   my job performance

	Training Needed Column 1 (Yes/No)	Importance of Training Column 2 (1:2:3:4)
1. Cultural and Social Class Differences in Parenting	_____	_____
2. Family Dynamics	_____	_____
3. Developmental Needs—Preschool	_____	_____
4. Social Case Histories	_____	_____
5. Family Structure and Roles	_____	_____
6. Developmental Needs—Infant	_____	_____
7. Social Work Roles	_____	_____
8. Theories of Human Behavior	_____	_____
9. Delinquency	_____	_____
10. Community Resource Coordination	_____	_____
11. Parent Effectiveness Skills	_____	_____
12. Treatment Plan Formulation	_____	_____
13. Case and Treatment Evaluation	_____	_____
14. Psychology of Family Aggression	_____	_____
15. Human Sexuality	_____	_____
16. Child Welfare Law	_____	_____
17. Person Abuse	_____	_____
18. Abnormal Behavior (Psychopathology)	_____	_____
19. Diagnosis	_____	_____
20. Client Rights	_____	_____
21. Use of Goals/Contracts in Treatment	_____	_____

FIGURE 4.2. (*Section C—continued*).

22. Psychological and Social Processes
    of Separation and Loss   _____ _____
23. Treatment Objective and Formulation   _____ _____
24. Educational Resources for Handicapped   _____ _____
25. Communication   _____ _____
26. Active Listening   _____ _____
27. Interviewing   _____ _____
28. Confidentiality   _____ _____
29. Problem Analysis and Decision Making   _____ _____
30. Child Rearing Practices   _____ _____
31. Child and Adolescent Psychology   _____ _____
32. Interpersonal Communication   _____ _____
33. Dynamics of Child Abuse;
    Battered Child Syndrome   _____ _____
34. Parenting   _____ _____
35. Case Dictation and Recording   _____ _____
36. Sexual Abuse   _____ _____
37. Developmental Needs—
    Latency Aged (6–10)   _____ _____
38. Developmental Needs—Adolescents   _____ _____
39. Counseling/Therapy   _____ _____
40. Client Needs Assessment   _____ _____
41. Single Parenting   _____ _____
42. Nonverbal Communication   _____ _____
43. Crisis Intervention   _____ _____
44. Title XX Regulations   _____ _____

SOURCE: Washington, Rindfleisch, Toomey, Bushnell, and Pecora, 1979.

sponses and reporting the frequency distributions. With samples less than 50, the median (e.g., the "middle score" or the number above and below which 50 percent of the cases or respondents lie) rather than the mean should be used as the mean is more affected by extreme scores. Frequencies of age, years of work experience, educational background, and the respondent demographic information can be summarized. For larger samples, computerized data analysis is more efficient and allows more sophisticated analyses.

In contrast to the first two survey sections, the

knowledge area section is more complex. For those items left blank, a zero (0) usually is coded. A 1, 2, 3, or 4 is recorded where a training need has been indicated and rated. Three of the most common data summarization methods are described below:

1. *Number of staff requesting training.* Add together the number of staff indicating a need for training in a particular area. Those areas checked by a large number of staff can be considered high in priority.
2. *Training importance.* Each area checked as a training need is rated in importance using a four-point scale. Those areas not checked by a respondent are assigned a "0." To calculate an average rating of importance for an item, add together the worker ratings of importance for each knowledge area (including zeros). Divide this figure by the number of respondents. This produces a mean importance rating for each knowledge area that can range from 0 (no respondent chose it as a training need) to 4 (all respondents rated it crucial to improving their job performance). For example, for a study of 126 workers, the importance ratings for the knowledge area "Family Therapy" could be summed:

Respondent ID	Rating of Importance
Respondent no. 1	= 3
Respondent no. 2	= 1
Respondent no. 3	= 0
Respondent no. 4	= 2
•	•
•	•
•	•
Respondent no. 126	= 1
Total importance rating	= 158

Dividing the summed importance rating for all respondents (158) by the number of workers answering that item (126) will produce a mean average score for the survey item labeled "Family Therapy" (1.25). Carry out the division to at least two places to the right of the decimal so that a ranked list of knowledge areas can be developed. Make a list starting with those knowledge areas with the highest scores. Less important training scores will be further down the list (see table 4.1).

3. *Areas rated as highly important.* A third measure of training need can be computed by counting the *number* of workers who indicated they wanted training at a "3" (important) or "4" (crucial) level for each knowledge area. This number should be divided by the total number of questionnaire respondents to compute the percentage of workers who intensely want training in an area. A list of knowledge areas can then be prepared that ranks those areas by the percentage of "3" or "4" ratings. For example, 25 out of 100 respondents might rate crisis intervention as a training need at a 3 or 4 level. When the crisis intervention percentage (25 percent) is compared to the percentage of staff who rated child abuse at a 3 or 4 level (65 percent or 65 out of 100 respondents), we find that child abuse is perceived as a more urgently needed training area.

A sample of results from the last two methods of analysis are illustrated in tables 4.1 and 4.2 respectively (Washington et al., 1979).

With minor modifications, knowledge-based surveys can be used with supervisors in order to identify the training needs of their subordinates. The results can be compared with those of subordinates. This

TABLE 4.1.
Rank order of worker training needs by mean score of importance.
(N = 126)

Rank	Knowledge Area	X^a
1	Psychology of family aggression	1.78
2	Crisis intervention	1.56
3	Child and adolescent psychology	1.46
4	Adolescent developmental needs	1.42
5	Adolescent treatment techniques	1.41
6.5	Abnormal behavior (psychopathology)	1.36
6.5	Parenting	1.36
8	Antisocial (sociopathic) disorders	1.32
9	Counseling/therapy	1.30
10	Use of confrontation in treatment	1.28
11	Treatment of involuntary clients	1.27
12	Family therapy	1.25
13	Psychological and social processes of separation and loss	1.24
14.5	Dynamics of child abuse/battered child syndrome	1.23
14.5	Communication	1.23
16	Family dynamics	1.22
17	Worker stress management	1.20
18.5	Child rearing principles (parent effectiveness training)	1.16
18.5	Treatment strategies/techniques	1.16
20	Delinquency	1.15
21	Cultural/social class differences in parenting	1.12
22.5	Treatment of nonverbal clients	1.11
22.5	Single parenting	1.11
24	Sexual abuse	1.06
25	Physical and psychological effects of illicit drugs	1.04
26	Reality therapy	1.03
27.5	Interpersonal communication	1.02
27.5	Physical and psychological effects of alcohol	1.02
29	Client needs assessment	1.01
30	Behavioral disorders	1.00

SOURCE: Washington et al., 1979, vol. 1, p. 118.

a. Mean scores derived through the summation of the ratings of importance of the subject areas (including 0's) divided by the total number of worker respondents.

comparison is useful in situations where workers may not be fully aware of their training needs, but it must be viewed with caution since supervisors are typically asked to report training needs for their subordinates as a group.

Strengths

A primary strength of this assessment method is that it provides staff development personnel with a list of specific job-related subject areas assessed in terms of worker preferences and perceptions of importance. This reduces the need for extensive curricula planning and facilitates the design of targeted training. In addition, the method allows staff development planners to assess training needs across task or program areas. A knowledge-based survey with about one hundred knowledge items requires less than one hour to complete and uses a format that is comprehensive yet flexible.

Limitations

While the knowledge-based approach is straightforward, it also presents some problems. One is that unless a job analysis study has been conducted or data from an analysis of similar jobs is used, there is no clear linkage between the requested knowledge area and specific job tasks. In addition, achieving the appropriate level of specificity for the knowledge areas listed in the survey is difficult. Some users may find that their survey contains too many global knowledge-areas that are impossible to incorporate in short-term training programs. Finally, the survey generally identifies training "wants." Proponents of the worker ability/characteristic approach, noted in the next section, believe that training needs must be defined in terms of worker inability to perform specific tasks, rather than in terms of worker and supervisor "wants" (Dickinson and Bremseth, 1979).

Worker Ability/Characteristic Method

Definition

In contrast to the knowledge-based method, the worker ability/characteristic approach to training needs assessment focuses on factors which hinder effective job performance (Dickinson and Bremseth, 1979). As noted in figures 4.3 and 4.4, this survey approach uses worker ability and personal characteristic statements to identify worker training needs by describing the degree of worker job hindrance for each statement. The survey focuses on: (1) *functional* skills that are involved in performing different work operations (e.g., communicating, analyzing), and (2) *specific content* skills relevant for a particular job or field of practice (e.g., crisis intervention theory, human growth and development) (Fine, 1979). These skills are reflected in a series of worker ability statements that combine worker tasks, specific knowledge areas, and generic skills (e.g., using conflict resolution techniques in treatment; developing a plan of action with a client that specifies time-limited objectives and a criteria for their achievement). These ability statements can be developed through the use of staff and subject-matter expert panels.

TABLE 4.2.
Rank order of worker training needs by the percentage of workers reporting a knowledge area to be high in importance.
(N = 126)

RANK	KNOWLEDGE AREA	Percentage of Staff Rating the Area Highly Important[a]
1	Family aggression	41.3
2	Crisis intervention	36.5
3	Child/adolescent psychology	35.7
4.5	Counseling/therapy	32.5
4.5	Adolescent treatment techniques	32.5
6.5	Adolescent developmental needs	30.9
6.5	Parenting	30.9
8	Delinquency	30.2
9.5	Communication	29.4
9.5	Use of confrontation in treatment	29.4
12.5	Psychological and social process of separation and loss	28.6
12.5	Child abuse and neglect/battered child syndrome	28.6
12.5	Family dynamics	28.6
12.5	Treatment of involuntary clients	28.6
15	Abnormal behavior	27.8
16	Treatment techniques	27.0
18.5	Interpersonal communication	25.4
18.5	Child rearing principles	25.4
18.5	Worker stress management	25.4
18.5	Treatment of nonverbal clients	25.4
21.5	Cultural/social class differences in parenting	23.8
21.5	Behavior disorders	23.8
24	Client needs assessment	23.0
24	Diagnosis	23.0
24	Physical and psychological effects of illicit drugs	23.0
27.5	Problem analysis	22.2
27.5	Parent effectiveness training	22.2
27.5	Sexual abuse	22.2
27.5	Physical and psychological effects of alcohol	22.2

TABLE 4.2. (*continued*).

32	Case management	21.4
32	Treatment plan formulation	21.4
32	Case/treatment evaluation	21.4
32	Single parenting	21.4
32	Reality therapy	21.4
35	Child welfare law	20.6

SOURCE: Washington et al., 1979, vol. 1, p. 117.
a. Importance was measured on a four-point scale with ratings between 3–4 considered highly important.

For each ability statement, workers are asked to rate how often they encounter situations requiring such ability and the degree to which a worker's current inability in that area (lack of knowledge or skill) has hindered him or her in the job.[5] The concept of job hindrance can be explained in the following way: "Each of our jobs requires a certain level of knowledge and skill. Sometimes, our job performance in a particular area may be hindered by a lack of knowledge and/or skill. For example, one might be very knowledgeable and skillful in working with children who are anxious or depressed. Yet at the same time, one might find that ability to provide services to an alcoholic parent is limited (hindered) by one's current level of knowledge and/or skill in that area. Thus the worker ability/characteristic survey can help us identify those areas in which our job performance is hindered by a lack of knowledge and/or skill."

The worker characteristic section of the survey asks staff to rate their level of job hindrance, but this section focuses on *personal* skills, which are skills used in managing the interaction of self with the work situation. These skills relate to personal or interpersonal competencies (e.g., making others comfortable in an

FIGURE 4.3.
Worker abilities.

The questions apply to many of the abilities you use in serving clients. These "abilities" refer to specific task-related competencies that have both *knowledge* and *skill* components. Please respond to each item by circling the appropriate number in each column. For those abilities that do not apply to your specific job, please place a checkmark in the space labeled "N/A" (not applicable) and leave the two columns blank.

Ability	N/A	FREQUENCY				DEGREE OF HINDRANCE								
		How often do you deal with situations requiring this?				To what degree are you hindered in performing your job by a current lack of knowledge or skill in this area?								
		Twice/ Year	Once/ Month	Once/ Week	More Than Once/ Week	Not At All								A Great Deal
1. Reviewing police reports to determine whether evidence is sufficient to sustain a delinquency petition.	——	0	1	2	3	0	1	2	3	4	5	6	7	8
2. Conducting a pre-hearing or pre-disposition investigation within a limited time frame by gathering data about the client's social/legal history, educational/medical status, and other information.	——	0	1	2	3	0	1	2	3	4	5	6	7	8
3. Knowing when to recommend revocation of probation or parole.	——	0	1	2	3	0	1	2	3	4	5	6	7	8

4. Determining and recommending appropriate types and amounts of restitution. ___ 0 1 2 3 0 1 2 3 4 5 6 7 8

5. Determining the appropriateness of a detention intake referral by using police reports, family background, case or delinquency records, personal interviews, or other information. ___ 0 1 2 3 0 1 2 3 4 5 6 7 8

6. Conducting or participating in case staffing with placement agencies, institutional staff, or mental health providers. ___ 0 1 2 3 0 1 2 3 4 5 6 7 8

7. Developing a supervision or parole plan for a client using case, family, comunity, and institutional input. ___ 0 1 2 3 0 1 2 3 4 5 6 7 8

SOURCE: Pecora, 1982d.

interview and tolerance of frustration). Respondents are asked to rate how satisfied they are with the extent to which they have each characteristic. For each item they are also requested to indicate how much each of their worker characteristics has hindered them in their jobs. An abbreviated worker characteristic section is illustrated in figure 4.4.

The demographic section of this survey is similar to the worker demographic and conditions of training sections of the knowledge-based method and gathers demographic information, worker perceptions of training incentives, barriers to training, and information about preferred training methods. Completion of all three sections requires less than one hour, and the survey can be administered by mail or in person to staff. In addition, with minor modifications, the worker ability and worker characteristic sections of the survey can be completed by supervisors who rate what they perceive to be the areas of job hindrance for their subordinates.

Staff development researchers believe that training needs must be defined in terms of *worker inability to perform certain tasks,* rather than in terms of worker or supervisor "wants" or perceptions of areas where "training could improve the worker's job" (Dickinson and Bremseth, 1979:2). This is a subtle but important distinction. In this context, a training need has been defined as an inability or projected inability to perform work activity based on a specific performance standard (Fine, 1979). Using this definition, training "needs" may be significantly different from training "wants" (Brown and Wedel, 1974).

Second, training plans should be developed by curriculum work groups composed of staff development specialists and worker/supervisor representatives. The function of the survey is to provide this group with an empirically valid data base for developing training plans—not merely to provide a list of topic areas. Finally, organizational and political factors substantially affect worker performance and must be considered when interpreting worker training needs or inabilities. It must be recognized that certain aspects of organizational or worker performance are not amenable to improvement through training. Thus, this survey approach helps to differentiate actual training needs from organizational barriers, resource limitations, or personal limitations (Dickinson and Bremseth, 1979).

Noncomputer Data Analysis and Use

As with the knowledge-based approach, manually calculating frequencies, percentages, and mean or median scores is possible. With ordinal data (scales of 0-5) the median is the most appropriate statistic. Worker hindrance rankings for each ability and characteristic item are the primary data of interest, as they pinpoint what worker abilities and characteristics are areas of training need. Frequency and importance ratings for each ability item can be used to rank training needs as well. The demographic section of the worker ability/characteristic survey is analyzed in much the same way as the knowledge-based method. Educational and training profiles of staff can be obtained, as well as their opinions about training incentives, barriers, and methods.

Computerized Data Analysis and Use

A combined rating for each worker ability item can be calculated by weighting the importance rating by

FIGURE 4.4.
Worker characteristics.

The following characteristics are shared by most people to one degree or another. Please rate yourself on each characteristic and indicate how it affects your job performance by circling the appropriate number in each column.

LEVEL OF SATISFACTION					CHARACTERISTIC	DEGREE OF HINDRANCE								
How satisfied are you with the extent to which you have this characteristic?						How has this hindered you in performing your job?								
Very Satisfied	Some-what Satisfied	Somewhat Dis-satisfied		Very Dis-satisfied		Not At All							A Great Deal	
0	1	2	3	4	5	96. Tolerance of frustration.	0	1	2	3	4	5	6	7	8
0	1	2	3	4	5	97. Perseverance.	0	1	2	3	4	5	6	7	8
0	1	2	3	4	5	98. Managing feelings of hostility toward a juvenile offender.	0	1	2	3	4	5	6	7	8
0	1	2	3	4	5	99. Feeling part of a helping team.	0	1	2	3	4	5	6	7	8

0	1	2	3	4	5		100. Handling negative attitudes and behaviors of others.	0	1	2	3	4	5	6	7	8
0	1	2	3	4	5		101. Feeling comfortable with what you know.	0	1	2	3	4	5	6	7	8
0	1	2	3	4	5		102. Ability to learn from your mistakes.	0	1	2	3	4	5	6	7	8
0	1	2	3	4	5		103. Image of yourself as a professional.	0	1	2	3	4	5	6	7	8
0	1	2	3	4	5		104. High yet realistic expectations of others.	0	1	2	3	4	5	6	7	8
0	1	2	3	4	5		105. Feeling that what you do on your job will make a difference.	0	1	2	3	4	5	6	7	8
0	1	2	3	4	5		106. Caring for your work.	0	1	2	3	4	5	6	7	8
0	1	2	3	4	5		107. Ability to be objective.	0	1	2	3	4	5	6	7	8

SOURCE: Pecora, 1982d.

the frequency with which a worker uses a particular ability. For example, if an ability item was used "hardly ever," it receives a weight of 2; "once a month" receives 12; "once a week" is assigned the number 50; and "every day" is given the number 250. Each worker's rating of importance for an area (0, 1, 2, 3, or 4) is then multiplied by their weighted frequency score (2, 12, 50, or 250). This produces a "frequency/importance" score for each ability item for each respondent. When these weighted scores are summed and averaged for all workers, a *combined* measure of frequency and importance is obtained for each ability. Thus, a survey item that is ranked high in terms of training need and importance may be ranked low when the rating of importance is adjusted by frequency of use. Although an optimum weighting system has not yet been developed, this rough weighting technique is described because agency administrators have found this type of information to be extremely useful in determining training priorities.

Presented in table 4.3 is an example of a summary table of a pilot study that presents worker abilities ranked by the median degree of hindrance for each ability.[6] The ability items can be ranked also by the percentage of workers rating an ability area as highly affected by some kind of hindrance. Standard deviation (Std. Dev.) scores measure how much, on the average, respondents varied in their ratings. This provides a rough measure of staff consensus about job hindrance.[7] Supervisor ratings can be compared to those of workers. The ability rankings could also be modified by ratings of importance or by weighted scores. Similar tables would be constructed for worker characteristic items. Agency reports should actually use a variety of tables so that a staff development planning group could easily compare the high priority areas for training based on each of the criteria mentioned above.

Strengths

The worker ability/characteristic needs assessment method has been successfully tested in public and voluntary social service agencies in a number of states.[8] The advantage of this method is that it addresses three types of skills: *personal* (interpersonal), *functional* (process), and *specific content* (knowledge application). Because the survey focuses on areas of job hindrance and not on training "wants," it provides a direct indication of those worker abilities where a lack of knowledge or skill has limited the capacity of the worker to perform the job. In addition, the survey format is flexible enough to allow supervisor ratings of importance and hindrance to be compared with worker ratings.

Limitations

This approach identifies worker and supervisor perceptions of areas of job hindrance due to insufficient knowledge or skill. One disadvantage is that ratings of (dis)satisfaction and hindrance may be biased because of respondent tendencies to rate themselves in accordance with the norms of the agency. While anonymous reporting may reduce this bias, there is no easy way of detecting its extent other than through comparison of worker and supervisor ratings or use of social desirability scales.

In addition, data produced from the survey are in the form of worker abilities or personal characteristics. A training-design group composed of staff develop-

TABLE 4.3.
Rank order of ability items by median rating of hindrance for social work staff. (N = 7)

Rank		Ability	Median Degree of Hindrance[a]	Std. Dev.	Supv. Rating	Reported by Allied Professionals
1	68.	Working with adolescent alcoholics or drug abusers.	2.67	.98	2.00	
2.5[b]	3.	Assessing the emotional and physical effects of neglect and abuse on children.	2.63	1.11	1.00	X
2.5	31.	Using written service contracts in working with clients and/or foster parents.	2.63	1.29	4.00	
4	57.	Understanding the unique characteristics of and working with Native American children and families.	2.50	.82	3.00	
5	63.	Working with children who have been physically or sexually abused.	2.33	.98	2.00	
6	35.	Knowing techniques for motivating a client to change.	2.25	1.35	3.00	
7	52.	Working with groups of adolescents.	2.17	.75	2.00	X

116

11	27.	Providing concrete child and adolescent behavior management techniques to foster or birth parents.	2.00	.82	1.00	X
11	14.	Understanding a case situation from different points of view, e.g., yours, the client's, the community's.	2.00	.82	1.00	X
11	73.	Understanding and using agency policy; contributing to the establishment or modification of policy.	2.00	1.22	1.00	
11	55.	Understanding the unique characteristics of and working with Black children and families.	2.00	1.57	3.00	
11	56.	Understanding the unique characteristics of and working with Hispanic children and families.	2.00	1.30	2.00	
11	62.	Working with children who are anxious or depressed.	2.00	1.07	3.00	
11	51.	Working with groups of birth or foster parents.	2.00	1.22	2.00	

SOURCE: Pecora, Dodson, Teather, and Whittaker, 1983.
 a. Degree of hindrance was measured according to a six-point scale with the following scale anchors: (0) Not at all, (1) Barely, (3) Somewhat, (5) Greatly.
 b. Tied ranks are alphabetically arranged.

ment specialists, subject-matter experts, workers, and supervisors is necessary to translate the data into training content and methods. Finally, some worker characteristic (interpersonal skill) items are exceedingly difficult to remedy through training (e.g., "Image of yourself as a professional" and "Taking risks").

Translating Needs Assessment Findings into Training Goals and Learning Objectives

Once the needs assessment data have been collected, the staff development manager in conjunction with a planning group needs to translate the data into training goals and learning objectives. For example, a recent statewide needs assessment determined that the following ability areas were rated high in worker job hindrance by a large percentage of workers and supervisors: (1) working with adolescents, (2) family-based practice techniques, (3) client motivation, (4) practice techniques for working with victims of abuse, and (5) adoption placement (see table 4.4). The area related to family-based practice techniques for working with neglecting or abusive parents was seen as a critical training need for some staff because of the rising child protective service caseloads due to the state's poor economic situation. A staff development planning group might subdivide this topic area into such components as understanding the causes of neglect and abuse, knowing techniques for motivating abusive parents to change, developing family support systems, teaching self-help and parenting skills, and developing behavior-specific case plans. Each of these subtopics could then be used to specify learning objectives for each part of the training session. For example, some of the learning objectives for developing family support systems might include the following:

1. Demonstrate ability to describe three different types of family support systems.
2. Using family interview notes or case record material, demonstrate ability to map a parent or family's support network.
3. Demonstrate ability to select three appropriate strategies for strengthening a family support network using case records and client interview data.
4. Demonstrate capacity to cite three strengths and three limitations of using informal helping persons, such as neighbors or friends, to strengthen a family's support network.

These learning objectives could then be used to develop specific resource materials, course lectures, training exercises, and training evaluation instruments.

The training needs assessment methods in this chapter have all successfully been used with state social service agencies. While the worker ability/characteristics method used in combination with allied professional interviews is preferred, logistical issues may favor the knowledge-based approach depending on the availability of information about job tasks and worker competencies. If job analysis studies have not been conducted or if only minimal job description information is available, staff development personnel may find it preferable to use a planning group to specify knowledge-areas essential for job performance. Conversely, if job analysis or service delivery research is available, or if time and resources permit more extensive planning, then construction of a worker ability/characteristics survey is recommended.[9]

TABLE 4.4.
Summary of worker training needs for state child welfare staff. (N = 216)

	Ability	Worker Rank[a]	Supv. Rank[a]	Freq. of Use[b]	Training Want[c]	Prog. Area[d]
7.	Identifying and serving adolescent alcoholics or drug abusers.	1	2	E**		
68.	Knowing how to manage job-related stress and how to revitalize yourself.	2	1	A	X	CPS
34.	Knowing techniques for motivating a client to change.	3	5	A	X	FC
72.	Recruiting and working with parents of "special needs" children (e.g., those who are physically or mentally disabled).	4	—	F**		
44.	Working with children who are anxious or depressed.	5	16	C		
49.	Adapting the helping process to the particular needs of especially challenging clients (e.g., children or adolescents who are hostile, passive, retarded, or extremely dependent).	6	3.5	C	X	
59.	Knowing when and how to terminate parental rights.	7	—	F**	X	I-H
2.	Assessing a child's cognitive, emotional, and behavioral development; identifying both strengths and weaknesses.	8	27	B	X	FC
37.	Having and using a theoretical knowledge base of family structure and dynamics.	9	22	B	X	

31.	Working effectively with involuntary or resistant clients.	10	6	B	X
45.	Using groupwork concepts or techniques to work with a group of clients.	11	3.5	F**	X
35.	Teaching self-help skills.	12	11	C	
36.	Getting beyond the crisis-to-crisis approach in working with a client.	13	17	C	
47.	Teaching parenting skills.	14	21	D**	X
50.	Using negotiation or conflict resolution techniques with clients or helping team members.	15	19	D	
29.	Working with children or adolescents who have been physically or sexually abused.	16	19	C	X

SOURCE: Pecora, 1982b.

a. Worker and supervisor ranks are from tables that ranked the abilities by median degree of hindrance.

b. Frequency of use (F) frequency of use: (A) More than once a week; (B) Slightly more than once a week; (C) Once a week or less; (A) to low (F) frequency of use: (A) More than once a week; (B) Slightly more than once a week; (C) Once a week or less; (D) Slightly more than once a month; (E) Once a month or less; (F) Twice a year or less.

c. These areas were reported by workers or supervisors when they were asked: "What are the two most important areas for worker training?"

d. A large percentage of staff from one or more of the following programs report the ability as an area of high job hindrance: (I–H) In-home services; (CPS) Child protection; (FC) Foster care.

** These abilities have a large number of cases that were marked not applicable to a respondent's job. This indicates that specialized staff may be reporting these items as areas of job hindrance.

— Rank for this ability is below 25 (worker) or 28 (supervisor).

The critical issue is the relevance of survey items to knowledge areas, worker abilities, or worker characteristics for effective job performance. Survey items need to be specific so that training curriculum can be easily designed. Subject-matter experts from universities, training centers, or research institutes can be helpful with the early stages of questionnaire construction.

Needs assessment as a data-gathering method requires rigorous attention to the definition of terms and the phrasing of questionnaire items. First, it is important to use a specific definition of what constitutes a "training need." Training-needs data should be scrutinized to identify actual training needs as distinct from attitude, resource, or system problems (Mager and Pipe, 1970). Second, survey or interview schedule items should be phrased in ways that avoid gathering data about training wants ("wish lists"). Third, staff consensus about specific training needs information is important, and criteria for decision making should be explicit. Thus, training content might be chosen by using one or more of the following criteria:

- Selected by the largest percentage of respondents.
- Reported consistently by one or more needs assessment methods.
- Mandated by recent judicial decisions or legislative changes.
- Necessitated by program or client changes.
- Perceived to be cost-effective or efficient.
- Perceived to be technologically most feasible.
- Possesses multiple effects by which training in one area improves worker ability or performance in other areas.

- Not addressed by job redesign or changes in the job such as more supervisory monitoring.
- Perceived to be politically most feasible.

A final issue is how the needs assessment data for a staff development program relate to the individual needs of staff members. It is important to be cautious about the extent to which aggregated training needs data reflect individual worker training needs. If a copy of a training needs assessment is kept by the worker and supervisor, they can jointly decide if available training opportunities will address some of the worker's most important training needs. The matching of individual staff members to specific training is generally an individualized process for all but the most basic of training.

This chapter has emphasized the importance of needs assessment for planning and implementing staff development programs. Six methods for identifying staff training needs were outlined: organizational performance analyses, critical incident studies, the nominal group technique, allied professional interviews, knowledge-based surveys, and worker ability/characteristics surveys. The last four needs assessment methods appear to be more feasible and were described in more detail.

Needs assessment methods are not a panacea for the difficulties connected with planning and conducting staff development activities. However, the methods in this chapter should provide staff development personnel and agency administrators with a foundation for making decisions about the most suitable method for building a data base relevant to the agency's staff development planning process.

Notes

1. Testing is another method of determining training needs. Results indicate gaps, if any, in the worker's knowledge or skill, which suggest training needs (Johnson, 1967). But developing written tests for social service staff that have adequate levels of content and predictive and construct validity is difficult and complex. One of the central issues is whether test items can be developed that discriminate between those staff who have the knowledge or skills essential for effective job performance and those who do not.

2. For detailed instructions on how to use the nominal group technique, see Delbecq, Van de Ven, and Gustafson (1975), and Rindlfleisch, Toomey, and Soldano (1979:28–32).

3. For an allied professional or key informant survey approach that focuses on the opinions of community leaders regarding available services and supports for training, see Rindfleisch et al. (1979:18–21, Appendix A).

4. For a more comprehensive description of the knowledge-based survey approach, see Rindfleisch et al. (1979), and Washington et al. (1979).

5. Respondent ratings of the importance of each ability item or the level of proficiency may also be incorporated into the survey design.

6. Future studies should use a 9 or 10 point hindrance scale because it results in more variation, enabling staff development personnel to more clearly distinguish ability areas rated high or low in job hindrance.

7. A more conservative measure of dispersion with ordinal data is the range of scores for a survey item (e.g., 1-2, 3-5, or 0-5).

8. See Dickinson and Bremseth (1979) for a detailed user's manual. Versions of the worker ability/characteristics method have been used with child welfare staff in four states (Green et al., 1979; Pecora, 1982a, 1982d), with administrators of programs on aging (Betz and Bremseth, 1980), and with juvenile corrections staff (Pecora, 1982c, 1982d).

9. For a comparison of the knowledge, task, and worker ability approaches see Pecora, Schinke, and Whittaker (1982).

References

Arkava, M. L. *Staff Development Training Needs: Assessment and Evaluation.* Missoula: University of Montana, Department of Social Work, 1979. (mimeograph)

Betz, P. H., and Bremseth, M. *Report of a Study to Determine the Training Needs of Management Level Staff of the Tennessee Commission on Aging.* Knoxville: University of Tennessee, School of Social Work, Office of Continuing Education, 1980.

Bremseth, M. K., Green, R. K., and Dickinson, N. *Assessing the Training Needs of Child Welfare Workers—A Self-Help Manual for Staff Development Personnel.* Knoxville: University of Tennessee, School of Social Work, Office of Continuing Social Work Education, 1980.

Brown, F. G., and Wedel, K. R. *Assessing Training Needs.* Washington, D.C.: National Training and Development Service, 1974.

Clegg, R. K. *The Administrator in Public Welfare.* Springfield, Ill.: Charles C. Thomas, 1966.

Delbecq, A. L., Van De Ven, A. H., and Gustafson, D. H. *Group Techniques for Program Planning: A Guide to the Nominal Group and Delphi Processes.* Glenview, Ill.: Scott, Foresman, 1975.

Dickinson, N., and Bremseth, M. *Assessing the Training Needs of Child Welfare Workers—A Self-help Manual for Trainers of Child Welfare Staff.* Knoxville: University of Tennessee, School of Social Work, Office of Continuing Social Work Education, 1979.

Fine, J. *Planning and Assessing Agency Training.* Washington, D.C.: Office of Family Assistance, Social Security Administration, 1979.

Green, R. K., Dickinson, N., and Bremseth, M. *Assessing the Training Needs of Child Welfare Workers—Project Report.* Knoxville: University of Tennessee, School of Social Work, Office of Continuing Social Work Education, 1979.

Huber, G., and Delbecq, A. L. Guidelines for Combining the Judgments of Individual Group Members in Decision Conferences. *Academy of Management Journal,* 1972, 15(2), 161–74.

Johnson, R. B. Determining Training Needs. In R. L. Craig and L. R. Bittel (Eds.), *Training and Development Handbook.* New York: McGraw-Hill, 1967. pp. 16–33.

Kirkpatrick, D. L. Determining Training Needs: Four Simple and Effective Approaches. *Training and Development Journal,* 1977, 31(2), 22–25.

Leonard, E. C. *Assessment of Training Needs.* Bloomington: Indiana University, Division of Business Administration, 1974.

Mager, R. F., and Pipe, P. *Analyzing Performance Problems or "You Really Oughta Wanna."* Belmont, Calif.: Fearon, 1970.

Magura, S., and Moses, B. S. Outcome Measurement in Child Welfare. *Child Welfare,* 1980, 59:595-607.

Maluccio, A. N. Staff Development in Child Welfare. *Child and Youth Services Review,* 1977, 1(3), 3-9.

Maveske, G. W., Harmon, F. L., and Glickman, A. S. What Can Critical Incidents Tell Management? *Training and Development Journal,* 1966, 20(4), 20-34.

Morrison, J. H. Determining Training Needs. In R. L. Craig (Ed.), *Training and Development Handbook* (2nd ed.). New York: Mc-Graw Hill, 1976.

Pecora, P. J. *Alaska Staff Development Project: State Report.* Seattle, Wash.: University of Washington, School of Social Work, Northwest Regional Child Welfare Training Center, 1982a.

Pecora, P. J. *Improving the Quality of Child Welfare Services: Needs Assessment for Staff Training in Alaska and Oregon.* Doctoral dissertation, University of Washington, 1982b.

Pecora, P. J. *Needs Assessment for Staff Training in Juvenile Probation: The Alaska State Report.* Seattle: University of Washington, School of Social Work, Northwest Regional Child Welfare Training Center, 1982c.

Pecora, P. J. *Oregon Staff Development Project: Assessing Worker Training Needs in Juvenile Corrections.* Seattle: University of Washington, School of Social Work, Northwest Regional Child Welfare Training Center, 1982d.

Pecora, P. J., Dodson, A. R., Teather, E. C., and Whittaker, J. K. Assessing Worker Training Needs: Application of Staff Survey and Key Informant Interview Methods. *Child Welfare,* 1983, 57(5), 395-407.

Pecora, P. J., Schinke, S. P., and Whittaker, J. K. Needs Assessment for Staff Training. *Administration in Social Work,* in press.

Rindfleisch, N. J., Toomey, B. G., and Soldano, K. *Assessing Training Needs in Children's Services—How to Do It.* Columbus: Ohio State University, College of Social Work, 1979.

Schinke, S. P., and Schilling, R. F. Needs Assessment and Child Care Staff Training. *Child Care Quarterly,* 1980, 9, 73-81.

Sundel, M., Homan, C. C., Lucas, J. D., Burt, G., and Clarren, J. E. *Local Child Welfare Services Self-Assessment Manual: Part 1—*

Checklists. Washington, DC: U.S. Department of Health, Education and Welfare, U.S. Children's Bureau, 1979.

Warheit, G. J., Bell, R. A., and Schwab, J. J. *Needs Assessment Approaches: Concepts and Methods.* Washington, D.C.: National Institute of Mental Health, 1977.

Warheit, G. J., Buhl, J. M., and Bell, R. A. A Critique of Social Indicators Analysis and Key Informants Surveys as Needs Assessment Methods. *Evaluation and Program Planning,* 1978, 1, 239–247.

Washington, R. O., Rindfleisch, N. J., Toomey, B., Bushnell, J., and Pecora, P. J. *The Project Report—A Report of the Ohio-Wisconsin Children's Services Training Needs Assessment Project.* Columbus: Ohio State University, College of Social Work, 1979.

Zober, M. A. A Systematic Perspective on the Staff Development and Training Evaluation Process. *Arete,* 1980, 6(2), 51–70.

Chapter 5

How Do Trainers Plan and Implement a Training Program?

THE ADMINISTRATIVE FUNCTION OF STAFF DEVELOPMENT includes the roles of program designer and implementor, as noted in chapter 1. These roles relate to the instructional function of staff development managers. The instructional function includes the roles of *translator* of training needs into learning objectives, *orchestrator* of training experiences, *facilitator* of the learning process, and *change agent* in relationship to individual and organizational needs. This chapter focuses on the range of instructional processes and techniques used in implementing a training session or workshop.

Translator

This instructional role relates primarily to the process by which a trainer works with line workers, supervisors, and administrators. Agency staff members can use assistance in translating job tasks that workers do not perform well into learning objectives. These objectives can serve as the foundation for individualized training plans. A skilled staff development manager should be able to assist staff in developing learning objectives for all levels of the organization. The process for developing learning objectives can begin with the training implications of new policies or organizational changes as well as with the specification of job functions related to service objectives and specific worker tasks. Supervisors are usually capable of identifying the knowledge and skill components of various tasks. If they are not, consultation with local university educators or experienced practitioners should be encouraged. Based on the perceived gaps between expected and current levels of knowledge or skill, specific learning objectives can be developed for different workers.

The development of learning objectives involves identifying current performance levels (what the worker is to be able to do), conditions under which the performance is expected to occur, and the acceptable level of quality of performance. As Mager (1975) points out, learning objectives provide a basis for selecting instructional content, evaluating the success of the instructional experience, and organizing a worker's own efforts and activities for learning (i.e., if you know where you are going, you have a better chance of getting there). Mager (1975) defines a learning objective as follows:

1. An objective is a collection of words, symbols, and/ or pictures describing one of your important intentions.
2. An objective will communicate your intention to the degree you describe what the worker will be doing when demonstrating achievement of the objective, the important conditions of the doing, and the criterion by which achievement will be judged.
3. To prepare a useful objective, continue to modify a draft until the following questions are answered:

(a) What do I want workers to be able to do? (b) What are the important conditions or constraints under which I want them to perform? (c) How well must workers perform for me to be satisfied?

4. Write a separate statement for each important outcome or intention; write as many as you need to communicate your intentions.

Verbs that are open to few interpretations are best. Mager (1975) cites the following examples:

WORDS OPEN TO MANY INTERPRETATIONS	WORDS OPEN TO FEW INTERPRETATIONS
To know	To write
To understand	To recite
To really understand	To identify
To appreciate	To sort
To fully appreciate	To solve
To grasp the significance of	To construct
To enjoy	To build
To believe	To compare
To have faith in	To contrast
To internalize	To smile

Appendix C has been designed to help you test your skills in recognizing good learning objectives.

The development of learning objectives is an important process in translating job requirements or tasks, training needs assessment information, and career goals into specific components of an individualized training plan. For some staff it may be easier to use specific worker behaviors as bases for developing learning objectives. With this approach, staff members describe present behavior and desired behavior and its consequences. The difference between these behaviors becomes the learning objective.

For staff development managers interested in developing specific learning objectives for use in workshops or individualized units of continuing education, a curriculum development model utilizing a task or cluster of tasks reflects one of the most systematic approaches to the development of job-related learning objectives (Hyer et al., 1971). For example, refer back to figure 3.2 in chapter 3 and review the task profile of the corrections worker; note that a cluster of tasks relate to giving and receiving consultation (e.g., numbers 13, 15, 16, 17, 19, 22, and 25). The primary actors in the consultative relationship are the client's family, other service providers inside and outside the agency, and superiors. The primary service goal could be as follows: Given a correctional worker's service delivery responsibilities to a caseload of clients, the worker needs to utilize effective case consultation techniques and procedures as measured by the use of information in the case records or derived from colleagues and the client's significant others. Three learning objectives related to these actions might be:

1. Demonstrate consultation and education skills in order to communicate effectively with client's family and significant others.
2. Demonstrate case consultation skills in order to gather and provide service delivery information to and from colleagues inside and outside the agency in order to improve services to a client.
3. Demonstrate the use of case consultation provided by superiors in order to effectively serve clients.

A trainer would then assess the worker's learning

needs in relationship to this task cluster, which constitutes approximately 25 percent of the job tasks, following methods described in the previous chapter on
needs assessment. The first learning objective may relate to the least complex tasks, while the remaining objectives could relate to the most complex tasks.

The systematic approach to developing job-
related learning objectives involves six steps. Step 1
relates to the selection of a group of tasks from an existing task profile or a profile developed by the trainer.
Task selection can be based on a critical component of
the job or recurring staff performance difficulties as
mentioned by workers, supervisors, or agency administrators. A service goal is developed in relationship to
the overall topic of case consultation. A service goal
could relate to a group of tasks that cut across a number of job responsibilities (e.g., interviewing).

In Step 2, attention is given to formulating specific
behavioral objectives that relate to the service goals.
These learning objectives can be formed by converting
the task statement into an objective by noting the
action verb (for example, "teach," "counsel," "ad-
vise") and the outcome phrase (for example, "in order
to accomplish X"). The key to framing learning objectives is to answer the following question: Given what,
the worker does what, evaluated according to what
criteria (Mager, 1968)? Additional behavioral objectives may be needed to satisfy the skill requirements of
a particular task.

Step 3 involves the identification of the level of
training to be conducted (i.e., starting where the
learner is, which is similar to the frequently stated dic-
tum of starting where the client is). Levels can be labeled arbitrarily as entry, middle, and advanced and
can signify the range of complexity within or among

educational levels (for example, community college, university, and graduate school). Whatever the delineations, special attention must be given to distinguishing between complex and less complex tasks as well as between the different levels of trainee knowledge and skill. Learning objectives can be developed with tasks as the anchor points.

Appropriate training procedures are selected in Step 4. These procedures address the issue of what the learner needs to be able to do or know: (1) identify the agency goals and objectives that relate to a set of tasks; (2) identify any instructions that usually accompany the tasks; (3) define the role and/or function that includes the tasks; (4) identify the performance criteria utilized to assess successful task completion on the job; and (5) identify for the learner the range of criteria commonly utilized to assess task performance.

In Step 5, subobjectives are written for each behavioral objective, specifying what the learner must know or be able to do before performing or completing the behavior objective. Since objectives based on task descriptions often encompass broad activity, they frequently lend themselves to further classification into subobjectives. For example, a specific training activity, such as analyzing and critiquing case conference reports presented as part of a case consultation process with colleagues, could be derived from the previous learning objective: to demonstrate case consultation skills in order to gather and provide service delivery information to and from colleagues inside and outside the agency.

In Step 6, the trainer assigns the particular type of training needed to achieve the behavioral objectives. Some objectives may be accomplished most successfully through a didactic lecture, in which specific content is presented. Other objectives may be best met by exercises that involve experiential learning (role play, simulation, games, and site visits). Still other objectives may require the application of content or experience acquired in another course or in field work.

Any learning theory or strategy can be useful for determining how the learner can develop the competencies reflected in each subobjective. Therefore, the trainer must have a working knowledge of the four major teaching approaches: (1) social interaction, in which participants learn through interactions with others; (2) information processing, in which participants translate environmental stimuli, data, and problems into understandable concepts and solutions; (3) personal development, in which participants seek to actualize their own potential; and (4) behavior modification, in which participants are rewarded for making appropriate behavior-shaping responses (Austin, 1981).

The final activity of the translator role is the compilation of the learning objectives and approaches into a description of an instructional program. Appendix D provides the outline of a guide for designing an instructional program (Lauffer, 1978).

Orchestrator

The role of orchestrator of the actual training process or workshop is based on the assumption that the trainer or staff development manager teaches participants very little, but instead, provides an educational environment in which participants are encouraged to learn and teach each other. A variety of instructional techniques can be used to build this educational environment, including lectures, demonstrations, films, guest speakers and panels, case studies, role playing, and simulations. For example, the trainer who walks into a training situation in which he or she knows very little about the personal issues that the participants hope to address in the workshop might want to use the nominal group technique noted in chapter 4.

Another technique useful for "breaking the ice" in a training situation where the participants do not know each other is called the resource hunt exercise. It is based on the assumption that all participants are potential resources to one another, inside the learning environment as well as on the job. The technique requires the trainer to gain pieces of relevant information about each participant or to develop a list of relevant job experiences that participants would be most likely to have acquired. These experiences are placed on a list as noted in figure 5.1. Each participant is given a copy of the list and asked to mingle with the others in order to secure the name of a participant who has had the specific experience. Sometimes humorous experiences are added to the list in order to enliven an otherwise serious information collecting exercise. In a matter of thirty minutes, a group of strangers can gain some familiarity with each other as well as written confirmation of the extensive experience base of the participants. The leader of a training session should be able to integrate the prior experiences of participants into the presentation of the workshop content, a key ingredient in orchestrating the learning environment.

For many staff development managers, the participant-oriented approach to orchestrating the

FIGURE 5.1.
Resource Hunt Exercise.

INDIAN CHILD WELFARE:
WORKING TOGETHER TO MAKE IT WORK

To begin thinking about the kinds of resources needed to best serve Indian children and families, we would like you to become familiar with some of the knowledge and skills each of you bring to your job and this workshop. Listed below are descriptions which apply to one or more participants at the workshop. Your job is to find persons who fit each description and have them sign their name to the left of the description. You have thirty minutes to complete the exercise.

_____ Member of Local Indian Child Welfare
          Committee
_____ Tribal Social Worker
_____ Has trained workers on working with Indian
          children and families
_____ Has arranged for guardianship of a child by
          an extended family member
_____ Has arranged for guardianship of a child by
          his/her tribe
_____ Has developed foster/adoptive homes for
          Indian children
_____ Is a member of the Yakima tribe
_____ Is a member of the Colville tribe
_____ Is a member of the Spokane tribe
_____ Is on friendly terms with a tribal elder
_____ Is familiar with resources for urban Indians
_____ Can recite the Indian Child Welfare Act
          in his/her sleep
_____ Was raised in an extended family
_____ "Troubleshooter"/Advocate for services to
          Indian children and families at the
          state level
_____ Has been a foster parent to an Indian child.

learning environment is preferred. Lauffer (1978:42) has identified several of the areas about which trainers seem to have some agreement:

1. Learners should be helped to find the connecting links between educational activities and the content of their experience and must be helped to recognize from the outset that integration and application of knowledge are the goal of instruction.
2. Learners should be encouraged to apply and test knowledge while they are learning and to test the validity of their experiences in interaction with instructors and fellow participants.
3. Instructional approaches should vary with the goals of instruction, the nature of the content, and the learning styles of the participants. Where appropriate, instruction might be content-focused, participant-focused, or problem-focused.
4. Learning programs should be organized to permit considerable freedom for the individual to accomplish his or her own objectives within the general objectives of the program. This freedom requires helping the participant to specify personal objectives and make appropriate selections of instructional format and content. In some cases it may require a considerable range of electives and independent learning opportunities.
5. No organization of a learning program is wholly satisfactory. Experimentation is desirable to uncover that pattern which best suits the objectives of a staff development program and the changing needs of staff.

Facilitator

The facilitator role can be played in at least three different situations. The first situation involves *brokering activities,* in which the staff development manager informs agency personnel about upcoming conferences, workshops, and certificate programs and courses. In addition, individual staff members may need assistance in assessing their learning needs and interests and thereby linking them to relevant resources inside and outside the agency. With such information staff can be notified about new learning opportunities as well as special staff development programs. A staff development library of books, journals, films, and training materials could be designed to assist staff in exploring new knowledge and skills.

The second situation calling for the facilitator role is the *leading of discussions* in a training session. Since training sessions usually stimulate a wide variety of personal questions and issues, the leader needs to be available for discussions in order to facilitate the learning process. In addition, some leaders like to establish a consulting hour within a workshop schedule for individual, small group, or total group interaction. Not only does this technique help to facilitate learning between the participants, but it also gives all participants an opportunity to learn about different methods for thinking through problems and modeling decision making. Appendix E includes a range of training techniques related to this aspect of the facilitator role.

Training session leaders can also facilitate individualized learning by scheduling debriefing sessions at strategic times, such as at the end of a morning presentation or at the end of the day. This is an opportunity for participants to identify their most useful learning as well as areas that need more attention or elaboration. Such sessions should be led in such a way as to help participants communicate with one another, not just with the trainer. This process can be facilitated by such questions as: Do others feel the same way? Do others have a different view? Are there specific ways in which additional learning could take place? These questions seek to involve the participants in shaping the direction of current or future training sessions.

One of the most upsetting experiences for trainers is the realization, part way into the workshop, that some of the material prepared for delivery is redundant in relationship to the participants' jobs, repetitious of some earlier learning, too simple for the level of sophistication of participants, or too abstract and theoretical. While the data that might lead to these conclusions is difficult to get unless every participant is able to speak up, it is generally true that one-third of the participants are clearly ready for the workshop, one-third are not ready and need more introductory material, and one-third are more than ready and need more advanced material. Knowing that everyone cannot be equally satisfied, the goal of the facilitator is to strike a "happy medium." This is best done by providing participants with at least two, and maybe three, learning options. By specifying a group learning experience in three different corners of the training room, participants can self-select according to their perceived needs and/or interests. The leader may need to momentarily "table" the workshop plan in order to acquire data from the discussion groups. The data can be used to modify some of the planned workshop content on the spot or to modify the agenda of the second workshop day. This experience may leave the leader with the feeling of being a ring master at a three-ring circus. However, the process is effective in drawing out the interests of a wide variety of participants as well as generating useful guidance for the trainer. It is counterproductive for a leader to rigidly proceed with the prearranged workshop agenda when he or she stands to lose two-thirds of the participants.

The third situation in which the facilitator role is important is after the training experience. Staff members should be followed-up after the training experience to gain their hindsight perspectives on the learning experience and the degree to which the new learning was applied to the job situation. The mere posing of the questions may serve as a learning reinforcement experience, in which the trainer or staff development specialist facilitates the continued learning of staff members. These issues will be addressed further in chapter 6 on training evaluation.

In order to perform the facilitator role, a manager must understand the range of *learning styles and teaching styles* as reflected in figure 5.2. These styles also help the staff development manager to seek some fit between the learning styles of staff members and the teaching style of a workshop instructor. The matching of learning and teaching styles is a rare event, therefore it is important to be alert to the different learning styles of workers in order to adjust the teaching style accordingly. For example, if the trainee population reflects both intuitive learners and explicitly structured learners, a combination found quite often among human service training groups, the workshop leader needs to include both task-oriented teaching activities for the explicitly structured learner and learner-centered activities for the intuitive learners.

In addition to learning and teaching styles, the workshop leader serves as a facilitator when he or she pays special attention to the climate in which the training is taking place. Ingalls (1973) has identified some of the *climate setting factors* in the following checklist:

PHYSICAL SURROUNDINGS	HUMAN AND INTERPERSONAL RELATIONS	ORGANIZATIONAL
Space	Welcoming	Policy
Lighting	Comfort setting	Structure
Accoustics/outside noise	Informality	Clientele
Decor	Warm-up exercise	Policy and structure committee
Temperature	Democratic leadership	Meeting announcements
Ventilation	Interpersonal relations	Informational literature
Seating: comfort/ position	Handling VIPs	Program theme
Seating arrangements/ grouping/mobility/ rest/change	Mutual planning	Advertising
Refreshments	Assessing needs	Poster, displays
Writing materials	Formulating objectives	Exhibits
Ashtrays	Designing and implementing activities	Budget and finance
Restrooms	Evaluating	Publish agenda and closing time
Audiovisual aids	Closing exercise	Frequency of scheduling meetings
Coat racks	Close on time (option to stay)	
Parking		
Traffic directions		
Name tags or cards		
Records/addresses, etc.		

Change agent

This final instructional role relates to an ongoing assessment of individual and organizational needs. In some ways, the staff development manager can serve as the in-house organizational development specialist. In order to be an effective change agent using organizational development techniques, the staff development manager must be able to assess the following issues for their staff development implications (Weiner, 1982):

1. *Agency goal alignment*—assessing the degree to which the formal, usually written goals match up with the informal goals reflected in staff behavior.
2. *Relationship of goals to staff activities*—assessing how well these activities accomplish the agency goals, how staff feel about carrying out these activities, and whether or not staff are doing what they claim to be doing.
3. *Task and process*—assessing the processes and procedures used by staff to accomplish tasks and the extent to which process issues hinder the accomplishment of tasks.
4. *Resources*—assessing to what extent performance difficulties are due to actual training needs (insufficient knowledge or skill) or due to insufficient service resources.
5. *Information*—assessing how much staff development information is available to decision makers, whether the information is sufficient for the efficient operation of the agency, and whether the information is sufficiently related for the agency's needs.
6. *Criteria for decision making*—assessing the usefulness of the criteria being used to make decisions about staff development.
7. *Informed choices and personal commitments*—assessing the degree to which staff have the opportunity to make real choices, based on valid information, and thereby feel involved in decision making and committed to courses of action which they helped develop.

The ongoing collection and processing of such data can be used to assess the fit between goals and activities, the tension between staff's desire for auton-

FIGURE 5.2.
Learning styles and teaching styles.

I. LEARNING STYLES

The incremental learner—proceeds in step-by-step fashion, systematically adding bits and pieces together to gain larger understandings.

The intuitive learner—leaps in various directions; has sudden insights; makes meaningful and accurate generalizations derived from an unsystematic gathering of information and experience.

The sensory specialist—relies primarily on one sense for the meaningful formation of ideas (visual, auditory, or kinesthetic).

The sensory generalist—uses all or many of the senses in gathering information and gaining insight.

The emotionally involved—relies on the emotional atmosphere of the learning environment to form ideas (use of drama, debate, etc.).

The emotionally neutral—relies on low-key emotional tone of learning environment, which is perceived as primarily intellectual rather than emotional (task-oriented, minimum emotive coloration of teaching behavior, etc.).

The explicitly structured—relies on explicit instructions, using clear, unambiguous structure for learning, with limits and goals carefully stated (feeling safe and at home in a well-defined structure).

The open-ended structure—relies on an open-ended learning environment with room to explore new ideas that are not explicitly preplanned.

The damaged learner—intellectually capable yet damaged in self-concept or feelings of competency in such a way as to develop negative learning styles (avoids learning, rejects learning, or pretends to be learning).

The eclectic learner—capable of shifting learning styles; finds one or another style more beneficial according to the situation (adaptive).

II. TEACHING STYLES

The task-oriented—prescribes materials to be learned and identifies performance criteria.

The cooperative planner—plans the means and ends of instruction with learner cooperation.

FIGURE 5.2. (*continued*).

The learner-centered—provides structure for learners to pursue whatever they want to do or whatever interests them.

The subject-centered—focuses on organized content in order to satisfy own conscience that the material was covered (often to the near exclusion of the learner).

The learning-centered—demonstrates equal concern for learners and curriculum objectives.

The emotionally exciting and its counterpart—shows intense emotional involvement by producing learning atmosphere of excitement and high emotion in contrast to subdued emotional tone; rationality predominates, and learning is dispassionate though equal in significance and meaning to the emotionally exciting environment.

SOURCE: Adapted from B. B. Fisher and L. Fisher, 1979.

omy and the agency's desire for control, the balance between a task orientation and a process orientation, and the fit between informed choice based on adequate data and staff commitment. The traditional areas of organizational development activity in agencies are leadership, decision making, problem solving, conflict management, communications, and planning. All of these topics can also serve as topics for development programs for staff at all levels of the organization. Staff development programming can serve as a form of organizational development and change provided that the trainer or staff development specialist understands the dynamics of the organizational change process. Resnick and Patti (1980) define the change process in terms of problem analysis, goal formulation and analysis of resistance, action system development and maintenance, formulation and implementation of a plan of action, assessment of the implementation decision, and the retrieval and transmission of learning.

A staff development manager or a staff development committee should be in a prime location in the organization to "take the pulse" of the agency. For example, group, organizational, and/or community problems surface in the context of a training workshop. Some of the problems relate to the attitudes of senior staff about the work of line staff, while other problems relate to current agency policies and procedures. Clearly there are limits to what a training session or program can accomplish. For example, preparing staff to improve their intake interviewing skills in an agency environment plagued with problems surrounding the utility of the intake policies, procedures, and forms can lead to considerable staff frustration. The information gathered informally from staff in a training workshop (with confidentiality guaranteed) can provide the basis for the staff development manager to explore the potential for change in the structure and processes of the agency.

The goal of this chapter has been to identify the critical instructional roles and skills required of a staff development manager. The instructional roles of staff development relate to the capability to orient, update, and upgrade staff by maintaining a balance between the needs of workers and the needs of the agency. More specifically, instructional skills relate to developing learning objectives, writing a description of an instructional program, using job tasks to develop skill training, using group techniques, assessing learning environments as well as learning and teaching styles, and analyzing the organizational change process. While the range of roles may appear overwhelming, each staff development manager must integrate the roles into his or her own work style and personality.

There is no one established approach to effective staff development programming. Rather, the combination of clearly understood roles and individual creativity and spontaneity are the key ingredients of a successful trainer or staff development manager.

References

Austin, M. J. *Supervisory Management for the Human Services*. Englewood Cliffs, N.J.: Prentice-Hall, 1981.

Delbecq, A. L., Van de Ven, A. H., and Gustafson, D. H. *Group Techniques for Program Planning*. Glenview, Ill.: Scott, Foresman, 1975.

Fisher, B. B., and Fisher, L. Styles of Teaching and Learning, *Educational Leadership*, 1979, 36(4), 245-54.

Hyer, A. L., Bernotovicz, F. D., Silber, K., Wallington, C. J., Kenyon, P., and Hale, P. *Jobs in Instructional Media*. Washington, D.C.: National Education Assn., 1971.

Ingalls, J. D. *A Trainer's Guide to Andragogy*. Washington, D.C.: U.S. Department of Health, Education, and Welfare, 1973.

Knowles, M. *The Modern Practice of Adult Education* (2nd ed.). New York: Association Press, 1978.

Lauffer, A. *Doing Continuing Education and Staff Development*. New York: McGraw-Hill, 1978.

Mager, R. F. *Developing Attitudes toward Learning*. Palo Alto, Calif.: Fearson Pub., 1968.

Mager, R. F. *Preparing Instructional Objectives* (2nd ed.). Belmont, Calif.: Fearson Pub., 1975.

Peterson, B. D. (Ed.). *Staff Development/Organizational Development*. Alexandria, Va.: Association for Supervision and Curriculum Development, 1981.

Resnick, H., and Patti, R. J. *Change from Within: Humanizing Social Welfare Organizations*. Philadelphia, Pa.: Temple University Press, 1980.

Tyler, R. W. *Basic Principles of Curriculum and Instruction: Syllabus for Education 360*. Chicago: University of Chicago Press, 1955.

Weiner, M. *Human Services Management: Analysis and Application*. Homewood, Ill.: Dorsey Press, 1982.

Chapter 6

How Do Trainers Evaluate Training Programs?

STAFF DEVELOPMENT MANAGERS FACE TWO MAJOR QUES-
tions as they implement and evaluate training programs: First, did training actually provide staff with
the knowledge, skills, or other competencies outlined
in the training objectives? Second, are the competencies and attitudes acquired in training being used on
the job to the extent that job and organizational performance have improved? Rarely do managers have answers to both questions, yet this information is essential for justifying and (re)designing staff development
programs.

There are at least five reasons why training evaluation is important (Chabotar and Lad, 1974). The first
reason is the need to determine if the training objectives that flow from organizational goals and service
mandates were met in the form of improved staff competencies. Training effectiveness can be measured in
terms of the amount of change in worker attitudes,
knowledge, or skills as reflected in on-the-job performance. A second major reason for evaluating training
is to identify the strengths and weaknesses of training
activities so that the quality of training can be main-
tained or improved through changes in curricula, instructors, method of presentation, educational tools,
setting, and other instructional factors.

Determining the relationship between training costs and agency benefit is another reason for evaluation. Costs in terms of staff time, materials, and travel can be weighed against such benefits as reduction of error rates, improved client outcomes, or more precise case recording. Alternately, cost-benefit analysis may be used to select various training emphases or techniques. For example, on-the-job training can be expensive in terms of the time involved in modeling, coaching, practice, and feedback, but skill retention might be higher than the learning gained in a less expensive training workshop (Chabotar and Lad, 1974). Thus, training evaluations may yield data not only about overall cost benefit but also about the relative merits of various training methods or emphases. A fourth reason to evaluate training relates to the need of agency administrators to justify training by using outcome data that documents superior staff performance or improved client relations.

The fifth and potentially most important purpose of training evaluation is to establish a data base for decision making. Evaluation data are useful in assessing the results of specific training programs and in determining the needs of staff for additional training. Furthermore, evaluation data enable trainers to assess the relative contribution of various programs and procedures in achieving organizational goals and objectives.

With these reasons for evaluation in mind, this chapter will focus on the evaluation of training program components (process evaluation), trainee experiences and performance while in the program (consumer and outcome evaluation), and post-training staff performance (outcome evaluation). Specific evaluation models and techniques will be described.

Training Evaluation Components

Selecting a framework for evaluation is an important first step in approaching the assessment of training. An evaluation framework, like the one in figure 6.1, can include such components as: (1) preliminary factors that affect the training program, such as the capacities of the trainees and the agency's service mandates; (2) the training program itself, with its objectives, content, instructional methods, and instructor; (3) trainee experiences and performance while in the training; (4) trainee performance after the program; and (5) the clients or consumers who receive services from trained staff. The arrows indicate feedback pathways into the program for its modification based on the results of various evaluation studies (Oglesby, 1975). While an agency ought to include all of the components in its training evaluation, most agencies focus on the second component related to evaluating the training program itself and the third component involving the reactions and performance of trainees while in the program.

Another framework for conducting training evaluations is presented in figure 6.2, and was developed by Fitzpatrick and Zober (Zober, 1980). This framework includes five stages ranging from pretraining input to the ultimate effects of training. The evaluation of a specific training program and its immediate effects involves the use of consumer satisfaction and knowledge, skills, and attitudes questionnaires. The effects of training are generally assessed through outcome evaluation instruments that focus on trainee application of training content and changes in job performance or service delivery. Irrespective of the framework selected, training evaluation includes both

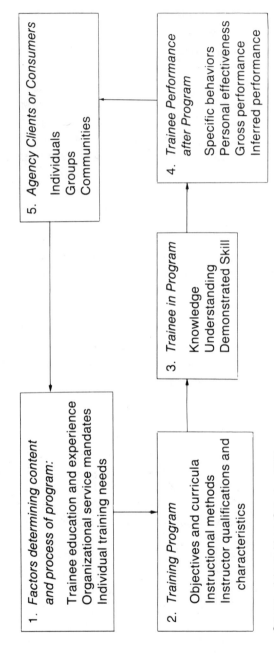

FIGURE 6.1.
A systems perspective for evaluating training.
COMPONENTS OF EVALUATING TRAINING

5. *Agency Clients or Consumers*

Individuals
Groups
Communities

4. *Trainee Performance after Program*

Specific behaviors
Personal effectiveness
Gross performance
Inferred performance

3. *Trainee in Program*

Knowledge
Understanding
Demonstrated Skill

1. *Factors determining content and process of program:*

Trainee education and experience
Organizational service mandates
Individual training needs

2. *Training Program*

Objectives and curricula
Instructional methods
Instructor qualifications and characteristics

SOURCE: Adapted from Oglesby, 1975.

process evaluation and outcome evaluation; the techniques for both methods are described in this chapter.

Process Evaluation of Training Program Components

The relationship between learning objectives and the training program represents one of the first opportunities to evaluate the training process even before it begins. How does the trainer link one or more objectives to a specific training activity? These learning objectives should be distinguished from broad training program goals that refer to the agency needs that will be addressed by the training (e.g., improve intake processing, reduce error rates). Several criteria for assessing learning objectives include: (1) relevance to the training needs of staff; (2) clarity and specificity; (3) relevance to the training program; and (4) relevance to the practice needs of the job, agency, and community. For example, a training session on child protective services might be evaluated in terms of the clarity, specificity, and job-relatedness of its learning objectives. Objectives such as "to provide a conceptual foundation of child maltreatment" or "to discuss legal issues relating to protective services" would be considered poor objectives. Conversely, learning objectives similar to the following are specific and therefore more useful for evaluation:

1. By the end of training, all trainees will be able to identify the presence of "doughnut burns" as a means of detecting physical child abuse.

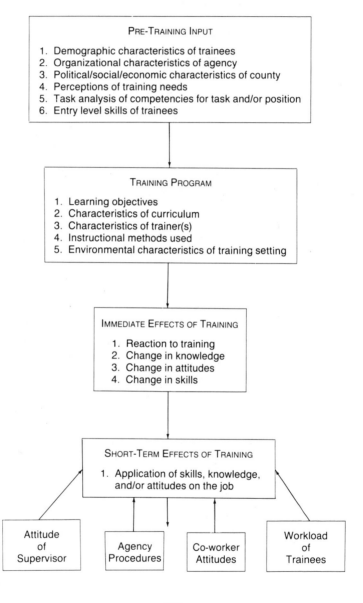

FIGURE 6.2.
*A model of training evaluation
components and stages.*

PRE-TRAINING INPUT

1. Demographic characteristics of trainees
2. Organizational characteristics of agency
3. Political/social/economic characteristics of county
4. Perceptions of training needs
5. Task analysis of competencies for task and/or position
6. Entry level skills of trainees

TRAINING PROGRAM

1. Learning objectives
2. Characteristics of curriculum
3. Characteristics of trainer(s)
4. Instructional methods used
5. Environmental characteristics of training setting

IMMEDIATE EFFECTS OF TRAINING

1. Reaction to training
2. Change in knowledge
3. Change in attitudes
4. Change in skills

SHORT-TERM EFFECTS OF TRAINING

1. Application of skills, knowledge, and/or attitudes on the job

Attitude
of
Supervisor

Agency
Procedures

Co-worker
Attitudes

Workload
of
Trainees

FIGURE 6.2. (*continued*).

SOURCE: Adapted from Zober, 1980.

2. By the end of training, 75 percent of the trainees will be able to describe four social or psychological factors commonly associated with physical child abuse.

The most common form of process evaluation is the assessment of learning objectives, training curricula, instructional materials, teaching methods, and instructor presentation. Is the training content job-relevant? Is a sufficient range of training methods or tools being used? Are staff members participating? In essence, process evaluation focuses on the aspects of training that may affect or determine trainee learning and subsequent performance. For example, in conducting a process evaluation of a training session on the latest *Diagnostic and Statistical Manual* of the American Psychiatric Association (DSM III), evaluation could focus on the relevance of the training examples for diagnostic activities using DSM III, the degree of ''match'' between the level of content and the abilities of trainees (beginner, intermediate, advanced), and the degree to which the instructor was able to promote meaningful trainee interaction.

Process evaluation is a necessary but, by itself, insufficient component of a thorough training evaluation because information about trainee application of new knowledge and skills to the job situation is not obtained. Thus, other evaluation methods are necessary to assess the quality and effectiveness of training.

Evaluation of Trainees as Consumers

The most commonly used form of trainee evaluation examines the relative satisfaction of trainees. Are staff satisfied with what they were taught? Was the length and format of training satisfactory (Schinke and Wong, 1978)? Consumer evaluation is generally accomplished through the use of feedback forms such as the one presented in figure 6.3. While this type of consumer evaluation is based solely on trainee reactions to the training, it is often the only form of evaluation used.

Learning Objectives Oriented Evaluation Instrument

A more structured and objective supplement to consumer evaluation of training has been developed

FIGURE 6.3.
A standard training evaluation form.

COURSE TITLE: *Children with Learning Disabilities* DATE: *January 1984*
LOCATION: *University Student Union* INSTRUCTORS: *R. Baer*

To guide us in planning seminars and workshops, please answer the questions below. You need not sign the form unless you so desire.

How would you rate the following?

	Excellent	Satisfactory	Unsatisfactory
Quality of presentation	_____	_____	_____
Adequacy of course content	_____	_____	_____
Length of course	_____	_____	_____
Adequacy of course materials	_____	_____	_____
Conduct of workshops	_____	_____	_____
Adequacy of facilities	_____	_____	_____

If any factor is rated "unsatisfactory," please provide explanation:

_____

_____

_____

What was of most value to you in this seminar?

_____

_____

_____

What was of least value to you in this seminar?

_____

_____

_____

Additional comments would be appreciated.

_____

_____

_____

SOURCE: Adapted from Fast, 1974.

157

by the Life Office Management Association (LOMA) and described by Fast (1974). This approach is based on two major concepts: (1) legitimate instructional objectives may reflect observable and nonobservable behavior, which can be measured by the training participant, and (2) the desired knowledge or skill, whether observable or nonobservable, should be assessed in terms of varying degrees of achievement rather than by an absolute yes or no measure.

The LOMA approach, reflected in figure 6.4, lists the primary observable and nonobservable learning objectives that are selected and rated by participants at the beginning of a training session. The trainee rates the importance of each objective by assigning 100 points among the objectives selected. For example, if three objectives are selected, the trainee might assign 50 points to one objective, 30 points to the second, and 20 points to the third.

After completing the training, participants then rate how well the training met each of the learning objectives they selected on a scale from 0 to 6 (degree of fulfillment). Multiplying the importance rating (1–100) by the degree of fulfillment (0–6) produces an "objective fulfillment" score. When these scores are compared for all trainees or summed across trainees, staff development personnel are better able to determine which objectives were important to trainees and how well they were met by the training program.

The completion of the LOMA evaluation form requires only a few minutes and has two important benefits. First, selection and rating of learning objectives helps to heighten the participant's awareness and recognition of how a particular training activity is meeting a particular learning objective. Second, when the evaluation form is redistributed at the end of the train-

FIGURE 6.4.
The LOMA evaluation form for rating trainee satisfaction.

LEARNING OBJECTIVES	DEGREE OF IMPORTANCE	DEGREE OF FULFILLMENT	INDEX OF OBJECTIVE FULFILLMENT
Check those that are important to you (_____)	Weight each checked objective for its importance to you, allocating exactly 100 points *among* all of those checked. A total of 100 points must be assigned.	Rate each objective you checked on a scale of 0–6 to indicate how well it was fulfilled. *	Multiply the importance rating by the degree of fulfillment score.

To be able to:

___ 1. Determine if physical child abuse has occurred. ___ × ___ = ___

___ 2. Write clear time limited case goals and objectives. ___ × ___ = ___

___ 3. Develop a client contract (etc.). ___ × ___ = ___

100   TOTAL = ___

*0-Unsatisfactory; 1-Poor; 2-Below Average; 3-Average; 4-Good; 5-Very Good; 6-Excellent

SOURCE: Adapted from Fast, 1974.

ing, the participants are brought back to the objectives they originally selected, irrespective of their impressions of the instructor or influence of the other participants. Thus the participants must evaluate the program in terms of specific, previously stated objectives (Fast, 1974).

The PRE-THEN-POST Consumer Evaluation Method

Another practical approach to consumer evaluation of training is the PRE-THEN-POST method (Mezoff, 1981). As with the LOMA approach, this method uses self-report measures by which participants rate themselves; but unlike other evaluation methods, participants rate their abilities at three separate points in the training process instead of just at the beginning and/or end of training.

What commonly occurs is that training participants overestimate their knowledge or skill prior to the start of training (pretest). At the end of training, participants realize how much they initially did not know or could not do. Thus their ability ratings at the end of training may be more conservative, thereby indicating only small gains in ability, when, in actuality, large gains were made.

For example, workers at the beginning of a training session on family treatment may rate their ability level in the area of client contracting as 6 on a 10-point scale. During or upon completion of the training, the workers realize that they actually knew very little about client contracting and now know much more. With this new awareness, they rate themselves at level 7 on the ability scale at the end of the training. If most workers react in the same manner, the training evaluation data would show an average gain of one point, when in reality the training may have produced more substantial gains in trainee knowledge and skill. This phenomenon, called response-shift bias, represents the tendency of training participants to revise their previous standard of judging themselves as a result of exposure to the training (Mezoff, 1981; Ralph, 1975).

To avoid response-shift bias, the PRE-THEN-POST evaluation method requires that trainees (after the training) reflect on their level of ability or functioning prior to the training and rerate themselves. This new measure of pretraining ability is called the THEN measure. Using the THEN measure helps to insure that the pretraining ability measure reflects the same yardstick that the participant uses for the post-test measure. THEN scores, which are rating of *pre*training ability made after training, are generally more conservative and lower than typical pretraining ratings. Because THEN scores tend to be conservatively low when they are compared to post-training ability scores, evaluations are much more likely to show a significant difference (assuming that training participants did in fact increase their ability through the training).

For example, staff development personnel evaluating a workshop on permanency planning for foster care might use the preworkshop rating form illustrated in figure 6.5, which lists the major instructional objectives and asks training participants to indicate their current level of ability with respect to each objective. This form would be completed by participants at the beginning of the workshop (PRE) and a similar form would be completed at the end of the workshop (POST). After completing the post-test rating form, the trainer would distribute a THEN evaluation form

FIGURE 6.5.
Examples of PRE and POST ability rating forms.

PRE

Participant Code No. ___

PREWORKSHOP ABILITY RATING FORM:
PERMANENCY PLANNING WORKSHOP

INSTRUCTIONS: Please rate your current ability (knowledge and/or skill) in relation to the following areas by circling the appropriate number.

ABILITY AREA (LEARNING OBJECTIVE)	LEVEL OF CURRENT ABILITY											
1. Defining "permanent placement" in foster care.	Low 0	1	2	3	4	5	6	7	8	9	High 10	
2. Writing time and goal oriented case plans.	0	1	2	3	4	5	6	7	8	9	10	
3. Describing the dynamics of attachment and separation.	0	1	2	3	4	5	6	7	8	9	10	
4. Documenting the appropriate steps for terminating parental rights.	0	1	2	3	4	5	6	7	8	9	10	

similar to one illustrated in figure 6.6. Participants are asked to think back to the beginning of the training and to rerate themselves as to where they think they were prior to the training in the light of what they now know (Mezoff, 1981: 59).

The data resulting from PRE-THEN-POST testing can be analyzed in two different ways. The most important way is to compare the THEN and POST scores

FIGURE 6.5. (*continued*).

POST

Participant Code No. ___

POSTWORKSHOP ABILITY RATING FORM:
PERMANENCY PLANNING WORKSHOP

INSTRUCTIONS: Please rate your current ability (knowledge and/or skill) in relation to the following areas by circling the appropriate number.

ABILITY AREA (LEARNING OBJECTIVE)	LEVEL OF CURRENT ABILITY
1. Defining "permanent placement" in foster care.	Low High 0 1 2 3 4 5 6 7 8 9 10
2. Writing time and goal oriented case plans.	0 1 2 3 4 5 6 7 8 9 10
3. Describing the dynamics of attachment and separation.	0 1 2 3 4 5 6 7 8 9 10
4. Documenting the appropriate steps for terminating parental rights.	0 1 2 3 4 5 6 7 8 9 10

as these represent the participant's subjective assessment of changes in ability over the course of the training. In addition, PRE scores could be compared with THEN scores to determine how much of the shift in reference occurred after participants were exposed to training. A simple comparison of PRE and POST scores, while possible, is not recommended, as this comparison is flawed because of possible participant

FIGURE 6.6.
Example of an ability rating form for the THEN evaluation phase.

Participant Code No. __

PRETRAINING RATING FORM:
PERMANENCY PLANNING WORKSHOP

INSTRUCTIONS: This questionnaire asks you to re-evaluate your ability level before the training began. Think back to the beginning of this program. Now that the training is over, how would you rate yourself as having been before?

You may remember how you rated yourself on these areas when you completed the pretraining form at the beginning. *Do not* simply tell us (from memory) how you *used* to see yourself. Rather, we want these ratings to be your current opinion of how you *should* have rated yourself (in light of your new understanding or skill). There *may or may not* be any difference between your pretesting rating and this reassessment. For example, based on your workshop experience, you might rate your previous knowledge and skill higher because you knew more than you thought, lower because you discovered that you had less than you originally thought, or about the same.

Your results will not be seen by your agency and your answers will be kept strictly confidential. So please answer as honestly as possible.

ABILITY AREA (LEARNING OBJECTIVE)	LEVEL OF ABILITY BEFORE TRAINING
1. Defining "permanent placement" in foster care.	Low High 0 1 2 3 4 5 6 7 8 9 10
2. Writing time and goal oriented case plans.	0 1 2 3 4 5 6 7 8 9 10

FIGURE 6.6. (*continued*).

3. Describing the
   dynamics of
   attachment and
   separation.   0 1 2 3 4 5 6 7 8 9 10
4. Documenting the
   appropriate steps for
   terminating parental
   rights.   0 1 2 3 4 5 6 7 8 9 10

SOURCE: Adapted from Mezoff, 1981.

response shift bias (Mezoff, 1981). The PRE-THEN-POST testing evaluation method has been shown to be superior in such training areas as interviewing and assertiveness skills training (Howard, Dailey, and Gulanick, 1979), human relations training (Mezoff, 1979), and traditional classroom learning activities (Howard, Schmeck, and Bray, 1979). In addition, this evaluation method is easy to administer, requires little modification of the rating forms currently in use, and documents training benefits which conventional evaluation procedures often fail to detect (Mezoff, 1981).

Evaluations Focusing on Trainee Performance During and After Training

The best evidence of a training program's effectiveness is the measurable changes it produces in trainee attitude, knowledge, skills, and job performance. There are many aspects of trainee performance that can be examined during and after training. They include: (1) opinions, (2) attitudes, (3) knowledge of facts or principles, (4) skills (newly acquired or improved behaviors related to the training), and (5) changes in job performance, such as personal effectiveness, job behavior, overall performance, and levels of poor performance (Oglesby, 1975). Changes in these areas depend, at least in part, on the quality of the training content, methods, and instructors as well as on the agency's organizational climate, supervisory support, and program resources (Mosel, 1957).

Ideally, the effects of training should be reflected in job behavior and trainee achievements. Measurements of trainee achievement are usually related to training goals and objectives. The challenge lies in specifying measurable training objectives so that staff development managers can measure training results against such criteria as improved service delivery, reduced operating costs, reduced turnover, or increased client satisfaction (Chabotar and Lad, 1974).

Because of the measurement difficulties associated with outcome evaluation, the next section will highlight some common approaches to outcome evaluation of training. Evaluative designs, outcome criteria, and model applications will be described.

Outcome Evaluation Designs Using Control Groups or Matching

A successful training evaluation seeks to isolate the effects of training from other factors in the learning or work environment, and generally requires some form of ''experimental control.'' One example of experimental control involves the formation of two groups, only one of which receives training at the time of the evaluation study. The other group (typically called the "control group") is trained at a later time or not at all. Ideally, staff members would be randomly assigned to both groups so that the groups would be statistically equivalent. For example, two groups of child protective service workers are randomly chosen from a public social service agency; one group is trained in the use of diagnostic procedures and the other is trained at a later date. Upon completion of the first group's training, both groups are assessed via paper and pencil tests, experimental simulations, and/or field ratings. The differences in diagnostic competence between the groups could be attributed to the training if extraneous factors such as those occurring during the training period could be ruled out or controlled statistically.

Another form of experimental control would use groups whose members are matched on certain characteristics (e.g., age, sex, education, work experience) that are thought to influence performance on the outcome measures. Again, the goal is to compare the effects of training one group with an equivalent untrained group so that the effects of training can be determined.

Outcome Evaluations Using a Pre-Post Design

Another approach to training evaluation is to measure staff performance before and after the training session(s). Trainers are able to judge the effects of training by means of one or more criteria (e.g., scores on an objective test, skill in a roleplay session, or employee error rates). Pretest scores help trainers pinpoint areas for special emphasis or coverage. Pre- and post-test designs are more feasible than other evaluation designs because a separate "control" group is not required. The challenge, however, lies in selecting clear evaluative criteria and measures that will be sensitive enough to detect changes in worker attitudes, knowledge, skills, or performance due to training.[1]

Other evaluation requirements associated with pre-post evaluation designs are validity (Do the instruments actually measure the appropriate areas of worker knowledge, skill or job performance?) and reliability (Do the instruments consistently measure the same thing?). Another problem that occurs is the confounding of change effects by extraneous factors such as the trainer's personality, changing work environments, or the "halo" effect, in which changes are due merely to participation in the evaluation study.[2]

An example of a pre-post evaluation design is the study of protective services training conducted by the Regional Institute of Social Welfare Research (Thomas and LaCavera, 1981). This study is notable because trainee control groups, pre-post trainee knowledge examinations, and pre-post supervisory assessments of caseworker skill were incorporated into the overall training evaluation design. Findings indicated that training was responsible for an increase in caseworker knowledge and skill. The evaluation data had implications for the design and implementation of training, as well as for altering supervisory practices and organizational policies.

Another example of a pre-post evaluation of training that highlights its utility as a means of testing a particular set of instructional techniques was a study conducted by Schinke and Wong (1977, 1978). Child care staff working in group homes for mentally retarded persons were trained using the behavioral methods of positive reinforcement, feedback, cueing (behavioral prompts), modeling, and behavior rehearsal. The training focused on improving staff knowledge of behavioral principles and techniques, staff attitudes toward residents, and job satisfaction. Multiple outcome measures were used to examine staff and group home resident behaviors two to three weeks *before* and two weeks *after* the training program. These outcome measures included a twenty-five-item objective knowledge questionnaire covering basic behavioral principles, techniques, and terminology; job satisfaction ratings; staff attitude ratings toward residents; and observational data on in-home staff/resident interactions. Study results showed an increase in child care staff knowledge of behavioral principles and techniques, and improvement in staff attitudes toward residents. The evaluation results also provide evidence that behavioral techniques can be successfully used to train child care staff.

The "Post-test Only" Outcome Evaluation Design

Another approach to training evaluation examines trainee knowledge or job performance only after training in order to determine whether or not training content is being applied on the job and job performance is at a sufficient level. This evaluation design is a "post-test only" design in that trainee knowledge, skills, attitudes, or job performance is measured after training has been completed and control groups are typically not employed.[3]

While the post-test only design is relatively straightforward, it is difficult to determine if something else, apart from the training, may have occurred that actually accounts for satisfactory levels of worker performance or the presence of specific attitudes or skills. In order to address this issue, the Participant Action Plan Approach (PAPA) was developed by the U.S. Office of Personnel Management (1980) to enable training evaluators to determine if and how participants changed their job behavior as a result of training. More specifically, PAPA enables staff development personnel to answer such questions as: What action plans have participants defined for themselves in seeking to apply the training to their jobs? What happened on the job as a result of carrying out the action plan? Do the action plans reflect the intent of those providing the training? What obstacle did the participants experience in applying what they learned to their job situation?

The PAPA method involves training participants in the development of "action plans," lists of behaviors that the trainees want to implement when they return to their jobs (e.g., involving more subordinates in decision making, writing more goal-oriented case plans). Ideally, the action plans are based on the training course. After one to four months have elapsed, participants are interviewed or mailed a survey to identify changes that they have actually been able to implement. The PAPA approach has five major phases: (1) preliminary planning, (2) in-course activities, (3) followup activities, (4) analysis and conclusions, and (5) report writing.[4]

Step 1: Planning for PAPA. This step entails determining whether the PAPA approach will fulfill the needs of the trainer, staff development manager, and/or the agency. Evaluating the specific data needs of the organization, estimating resources required to conduct the evaluation, and scheduling preliminary tasks comprise the bulk of activities for this step.

Step 2: In-course Activities. This step consists of two stages: (1) introducing PAPA to participants and encouraging them to think about ways in which they can apply the training content to their jobs; and (2) at the end of training, requesting participants to write action plans from the ideas generated in the training event which can be applied to their job situation.

The ideas generated during the training session can be noted on a form similar to figure 6.7. The ideas are then translated at the end of the training session

FIGURE 6.7.
Handout for recording ideas for action items.

IDEAS FOR ACTION ITEMS

Course _____ Dates _____

Ideas I would like to try out when I return to work, based on what I
learned in this course. _____
_____
_____
_____
_____
_____
_____
_____
_____

NOTE: You can use the workshop objectives, new insights acquired
      from the new content, the workshop handouts, or
      conversations with others to come up with ideas.

_____

SOURCE: U.S. Office of Personnel Management, 1980.

into action plans as noted in figure 6.8. Participants are given guidelines for writing clear and behaviorally specific action items by using such action verbs as describe, write, demonstrate, evaluate, remove, choose, and recommend. The guidelines encourage participants to note the time frame for implementing each

FIGURE 6.8.
Example of a completed action plan from a supervisory management workshop.

Course Title Supervisory Management
Name Dennis W. Kramer
Dates April 5-9, 1982

ACTION ITEMS	START TO IMPLEMENT		
I Plan to	Within 1 Month	After 1 Month	As Arises
Introduce the Nominal Group Technique to my staff as a problem-solving method.	X		
Devise a task profile for myself to more accurately describe my job.		X	
Review the job descriptions of my supervisees in order to assess whether the descriptions accurately describe their jobs.	X		
Seek to identify when staff conflicts are the result of organizational vs. interpersonal factors.			X

SOURCE: Adapted from U.S. Office of Personnel Management, 1980.

item (e.g., as arises, within one month, after four months).

To aid participants in selecting and evaluating action items, it is recommended that participants form groups of two or three so that each participant can share and clarify each of their action items. Each action item can be assessed in term of its clarity and specificity, resources necessary to implement it, implementation steps and actors, possible effects of implementing the action item, and finally, organizational supports and constraints.

Step 3: Follow-up Activities. Two to six months after the completion of the training event, participants are either interviewed or mailed a questionnaire in order to determine how training has influenced their jobs. Participants are asked to identify which of their action items they have implemented and what other new activities they have tried as a result of having attended training. The results (positive or negative) are sought and the supportive and constraining factors relevant to implementing each action item are identified. A sample interview guide is noted in figure 6.9, and users of the PAPA method are advised to read the PAPA manual as it contains a variety of helpful implementation tips and checklists (U.S. Office of Personnel Management, 1980).

Step 4: Analysis and Conclusions. In this step, data collected by interview or questionnaire in the followup are sorted, categorized, and displayed to show what items were chosen, specific behaviors related to each item that were implemented, a judgment of the outcome, and participant problems and concerns. PAPA data

FIGURE 6.9.
Interview guide for PAPA evaluation method.

DIRECTIONS:

This attachment contains suggested questions to be asked during the interview. Probes for getting very specific information follow the initial questions. Use them as appropriate. Space is provided below the questions for recording the participants' answers.

Course _____ Today's Date _____

Does participant have action plan? _____

Name _____

GUIDE FOR THE INTERVIEWER:

This is (*your name*) from (*name of your office*). We talked (*say when*) and arranged to discuss your action plan.

Is this still a good time?

Do you have your action plan from the (*name of course*) course in front of you? (If "No") Can you get it now? (If "No") We can work from my copy.

What I'd like to do is go through the items you wrote down at the end of that course and ask you some questions about them. Then you can bring up anything we might have missed, including any behaviors resulting from training that were not on your action plan.

(Make sure answers are specific enough so that you can envision the behavior being described.) Let's start with the action item that says, _____

_____

Have you been able to do this yet?

1. (If "Yes," Then use these STANDARD PROBES, as appropriate; if "No"—go to #2.)

   - Could you tell me more about that? What was the result?
   - Could you give me an example of that? What was the result?
   - How would you characterize the result? Was it positive?
   - Was it negative? Did it have both positive and negative aspects?
   - How did you carry that out? Who was involved? Have you been to the course? What was the result?
   - Have you done that more than once? Any difference each time?

FIGURE 6.9. (*continued*).

- How is that different from before?
- Were there any problems in carrying that out? What were they?
- Will you continue to do this? Do you foresee any problems?

RECORD ANSWERS BELOW:

What (with examples)?:

Result?:

How characterized (positive, negative, mixed, unknown)?:

Before?:

Problems?:

2. (If "No," then use these probes, as appropriate.)

- Why do you think that was the case?
- Any other reason you can think of?
- If (*problem*) had not occurred, do you think you could have done that?
- Are you still interested in doing this?
- If so, how do you think you can make it happen? Foresee any problems?

RECORD ANSWERS BELOW:

Why not?:

Other reasons:

Still interested?:

Can you make it happen?:

(If appropriate, use previously developed questions to relate behaviors to learning objectives.)

3. O.K., we've been talking about _____
   Have you done anything (else) similar to this? If "Yes," use standard probes listed under #1.)

(Repeat questions #1–3 for each action item.)

4. We've talked about your specific action items. Is there anything else that you are doing differently on your job since attending

FIGURE 6.9. (*continued*).

the course that you think is due, directly or indirectly, to your being in that course? (If "Yes," use standard probes listed under #1.)

Anything else?

5. Is there any way you think the course should be changed, to make it more useful to you on your job?

Anything else?

6. (Optional) What do you think about writing an action plan at the end of the course? Did it help you apply what you've learned?

7. (Optional) What do you think about this follow-up?

can be analyzed and organized in any number of ways, depending upon the data needs of the organization. For example, the action items and outcomes for all training participants could be categorized into common themes. Alternately, the behaviors included in each action item could be grouped according to the learning objectives for the training. One straightforward method for combining information from all or many participants into one chart is to use a "matrix analysis" of the action items, which groups them into common categories. Figure 6.10 is an example of such a summary analysis from a recent supervisory workshop. It summarizes the action plan outcome data related to "Organizational and Interpersonal Conflict Management." The descriptive narrative that discusses that section is presented in figure 6.11 to provide a concrete illustration of some of the conclusions and references that can be drawn from interview data when summarized in such a matrix.

Step 5: The Report. The findings of the PAPA evaluation are compiled into a written or oral report that can be used by staff development and administrative personnel to restructure training content, design new training programs, or address some of the intervening factors mentioned earlier (e.g., supervisory and co-worker supports, communication patterns, organizational policies).

Strengths of the PAPA Approach

One advantage of PAPA is that it can be applied to any training situation irrespective of content or instructional technique. No precourse measures or tests are required, and outcome data can be obtained on the following: (1) participant *reactions to training* related to likes and dislikes; (2) *learning* related to knowledge, skills, and attitudes acquired during training; and (3) *results* related to the impact of training on the participant's job performance and work environment (Office of Personnel Management, 1980).

By formulating action plans, trainees tend to focus their learning during the actual training event and are more likely to apply what they have learned on the job. A recent review of both laboratory and field studies found that the development of specific action plans through goal-setting affected task performance by focusing attention, mobilizing effort, increasing persistence, and motivating strategy development (Locke, Shaw, Saari, and Latham, 1981). Finally, training participants generally appreciate the follow-up interviews as they help to reinforce the training objectives by encouraging staff to apply what they have learned and addressing what they may have forgotten.

FIGURE 6.10.
Matrix analysis of evaluation data gathered using the PAPA method.

ORGANIZATIONAL/INTERPERSONAL CONFLICT MANAGEMENT

PARTICIPANT'S ACTION ITEMS	BEHAVIORS	OUTCOMES	PROBLEMS	JUDGMENT OF OUTCOMES		
				+	−	+/−
Handle conflicts	No action	No opportunity Still interested				
Use methods brought out in exercises for dealing with hostility, defensiveness, and evasiveness in office	Spoke to staff members individually, encouraging them to be more direct	Office environment has improved considerably		X		
Analyze in written form utilizing organizational/interpersonal model	Wrote up the approach and analyzed it	Not helpful now. The analysis was helpful and will utilize strategy in future	Budget emergencies keep staff from discussing anything but emergencies			X
Examine my own conflict management skills to assess my effectiveness with organizational and/or interpersonal conflict issues	Consciousness of issues has been raised. Taking "time-outs" often after working on problem to think through the dynamics	More effective and confident in ability to manage, more sophisticated with strategy now	Always problems when dealing with unpleasant tasks, but no specific problems with strategy	X		

Action plan item	Implementation	Outcome	Problems encountered		
Delineate whether conflicts are of an organizational vs. interpersonal nature	Immediately after the training, sat down with staff members and discussed problems, repeated problems back to staff members, and reflected on situations together	Some staff left their jobs	Staff member not wanting to talk about problem; staff member afraid to bother supervisor with problem; staff member feeling she/he could handle the problem his/herself	X	
Assess conflict using interpersonal/organizational conflict criteria and become clearer regarding staff's and supervisor's responses	Two supervisors differed on whether one problem was interpersonal or organizational; conflict resolved with counseling staff but no agreement was reached with two supervisors	Two staff resigned			X
(Not an action plan item but result of the training)	Handles conflict differently, listens more carefully, and seeks clarification	Groups have come to consensus following non-threatening requests for clarification on both sides of disagreement	No problems because doesn't become involved in "sticky situations"	X	
Conflict management	A new grievance procedure was established which makes the supervisors less reluctant to become involved in staff conflicts	Mixed outcome. Some supervisors are afraid of losing their independence in the quarterly review process			X

SOURCE: Carey et al., 1981.

FIGURE 6.11.
A descriptive narrative for a matrix analysis of section item data.

NARRATIVE SUMMARY OF ACTION ITEMS RELATING TO ORGANIZATIONAL AND INTERPERSONAL CONFLICT MANAGEMENT

Analysis of Matrix

The issue of conflict management was the theme singled out most often (N = 13) in the evaluated action items. One individual did not cite "managing conflict" as an area to directly pursue following the training, but found herself utilizing conflict management techniques as a result of the workshop nonetheless. This is important to note because it indicates that this element of the training left a vivid impression on several participants. Of those who planned to utilize conflict management skills, only two took no action when they returned to their jobs. The number of people interested in conflict management emphasizes the need for training in this skill area. For those who implemented their action items, few (N = 4) met with any problems. Two individuals did not experience any problems in attempting the new behavior. Two people who experienced problems overcame their obstacles and went on to judge their outcome as positive. Seven of the eleven people who took action experienced positive to "very positive" results.

Training Implications

The resounding response to this topic may point to the great need for training in this area. The responsiveness may also reflect that the ideas were new and innovative to this population. The vocabulary that many participants chose in phrasing their action items indicates that they had to go back to square one with the idea of creatively dealing with conflict (e.g., write, identify, analyze). Three trainees apparently overlooked (or didn't understand) "conflict management" or "handle conflict." This represents a lack of understanding of the larger issues dealing with interpersonal/organizational conflict management, perhaps pointing to a need for more in-depth definitions of the ideas during the training. One trainee simply stated, "unsure of how to identify between organizational and interpersonal problems." A problem with definitions might also explain some of the discrepancy

FIGURE 6.11. (continued).

between the behavior the trainees suggested they attempted in response to the action items. Of the six action items related specifically to understanding "interpersonal/organizational" conflict, only one trainee actually followed through on dealing with the issue directly. The others became involved in conflict resolution skills but did not directly address "interpersonal/organizational" ideas. It appears that this element of the training did not translate as well back to the job, but it may simply have been a problem with definitions.

One final interesting point is that the budget crisis was the issue underlying the barriers which the participants encountered in implementing their action items. It was discovered that the office of one trainee was in such a state of constant conflict as a result of budget problems that she was unable to implement newly found conflict management skills. It is ironic that a situation which constantly calls for these skills could be the barrier for their development. One training implication could be the need for instruction on budget-specific conflict management. In summary, functional conflict management behavior development was a well-received training topic. For those that attempted tasks back on the job in this area, two-thirds experienced positive results.

SOURCE: Carey, Cusack, Martin, Rose, and Wilson, 1981.

Limitations of the PAPA Approach

PAPA evaluations generally rely upon trainee self-report measures, which may be inaccurate. Although additional supervisory or peer reports are sometimes used to measure outcome, these do not wholly substitute for more rigorous measures such as objective tests or job performance data (e.g., changes in error rates or client outcome). Nevertheless, the PAPA method's simplicity, efficiency, wide applicability, and "built-in" trainee motivators (action items) constitute important reasons for considering the use of this evaluation method.

Linking Training Evaluation Findings to Service Outcome Issues

The data collected using PAPA or other evaluation methods can be used to evaluate changes in worker performance only if training objectives are made clear to the training participants at the start of training. For example, a training session on permanency planning in foster care might be designed and introduced to staff in the following manner: "This training is designed to provide you with a knowledge of permanency planning concepts and placement options as well as specific skills in developing time and goal-oriented placement plans and writing behavior-specific client contracts. As a result of this training you should be able to increase the percentage of permanently placed children in your caseload (returned home, adoption, guardianship, planned long-term foster care)." In the case of the PAPA evaluation method, participant action plans should reflect this training focus and the follow-up data should document staff successes, difficulties, and failures in applying training content to the job situation.

Training evaluation can provide information about improvements in agency service outcomes. For example, public or voluntary agencies may follow the example set by the Oregon and Alameda projects (Emlen, Lahti, Downs, McKay, and Downs, 1977; Stein, Gambrill, and Wiltse, 1978). These projects involved the training of a group of foster care staff in problem-solving skills by using goal-oriented and behavior-specific client contracts in order to increase caseworker and collateral services to birth parents through systematic case planning (e.g., early parental decision making regarding their child, delineation of parent and worker tasks and roles, facilitation of parental visitation). For each child who is returned home or adopted as a result of the training, the state would save at least $2,500 in foster care payments for every year each child would have been in foster care. While the Alameda and Oregon Permanency Planning projects did not distinguish the effects of training from the effects of more intensive casework services, results from both studies indicate that training staff in these areas significantly improved agency effectiveness in foster care.

In many areas of the social services, the benefits received through improved agency effectiveness greatly outweigh the unit or per staff costs associated with training an individual worker. One model for determining the value of training uses measures of change in individual worker or agency performance (Phillips, 1974; Seppala, 1978). This model allows a staff development manager to calculate the value of a training program by carefully comparing the full costs of training with the economic benefits achieved through improved worker or agency performance. For example, a voluntary adoption agency recently developed and implemented training on permanency planning and adoptive home recruitment for developmentally disabled children. The total cost for the training, including staff time, totaled $6,000, or $300 per staff member (twenty staff were trained).

A careful pre-post training evaluation might find that a higher number of children were placed in adoptive homes because of the training program. Major areas of agency savings include potential savings in staff time spent providing casework services to children in foster care and reduction of foster home costs because these children are placed in adoptive homes. If the average foster care costs for a developmentally disabled child are about $4,307 per year, it is estimated that subsidized adoption for that child would cost $3,360—a savings of $947 or 22 percent a year. If the training evaluation reveals that two additional children are placed by half of the trained workers as a result of the training, the cost savings are substantial, if we assume that fully one-half of those children would have otherwise remained in foster care until age eighteen. For example, if ten of the trained staff each placed an additional two children (average age twelve) in adoptive homes, half of which would have remained in foster care until age eighteen, a cost savings in foster care maintenance payments would be $56,820 (ten children × $947 savings per year × six years).

These savings ($56,820) minus the total cost of training ($6,000) equals the *net value* of the training ($52,820). This net value figure ignores the *social benefits* gained by the children and society through their permanent placement in adoptive homes and assumes that the effects of training would last only one year rather than result in workers placing two additional children for the next two or three years.[5]

This chapter has described the various approaches to evaluating training goals and learning objectives, trainee experience while in training, and trainee performance both during and after training. While outcome evaluation of trainee performance using control group and pre-post designs was emphasized, it is recognized that many staff development personnel lack the necessary time, resources, or expertise to use these approaches. Consequently, a special emphasis was given to the PAPA evaluation method, which focuses on training-related action plans and the experiences of participants in applying new learning on the job. Ideally more than one approach to evaluation should be used to assess process and outcome. However, if resources are limited, outcome evaluation should take precedence over process evaluation.

Notes

1. For information about developing and implementing client outcome monitoring systems, see Margo Koss, *Social Services: What Happens to the Clients?* (Baltimore, Md.: Urban Institute Press, 1979).

2. For more information on experimental designs and threats to reliability and validity, see Campbell and Stanley (1963), Chabotar and Lad (1974), Cook and Campbell (1979), Haynes (1978), and Nunnally (1978). Time series methods can also be used to evaluate training programs. See Cook and Campbell, 1979.

3. See Petty and Bruning (1980) for a type of post-test only evaluation study that investigated the relationship between type of agency training and employee error rates in the public welfare programs of aid to families with dependent children, medicaid, and food stamps.

4. For more information about the PAPA approach to evaluation, see an excellent users manual published by the United States Office of Personnel Management entitled: *Assessing Changes in Job Behavior Due to Training: A Guide to the Participant Action Plan Approach.* This manual is available from the U.S. Government Printing Office, Washington, D.C. 20402 (Stock Number: 006-000-01130-6). See Zober, Seipel, and Skinner (1982) for application of the PAPA method in a social science department; and Bremseth, Betz, and Prevot for an evaluative study that collected data from three steps in the learning process: "Reaction," "Learning," and "Behavior."

5. For discussion purposes, this cost-benefit example has been greatly simplified. A rigorous cost-benefit analysis would specify as many cost and benefit factors as possible, such as the present-value of the foster care savings, the length of the payback period, and changes in savings or performance over time. See Buxbaum (1981) and Young and Allen (1977).

References

Bremseth, M. D., Betz, P. D., and Prevot, C. Data-Based Comparisons of the Effectiveness of Current Evaluations of Research Strategies. In R. L. Edwards and T. R. Morton (Eds.), *Training in the Human Services*, Vol. 2, Knoxville, Tenn.: University of Tennessee School of Social Work, 1978.

Buxbaum, C. B. Cost-Benefit Analysis: The Mystique versus the Reality. *Social Service Review*, 1981, 55(3), 453–71.

Campbell, D. T., and Stanley, J. C. *Experimental and Quasi-Experimental Designs for Research.* Chicago: Rand McNally, 1966.

Carey, B., Cusack, R., Martin, J., Rose, P., and Wilson, S. *PAPA Summary.* Unpublished manuscript, University of Washington, School of Social Work, 1981.

Chabotar, K. J., and Lad, L. J. *Evaluation Guidelines for Training Programs.* East Lansing: Michigan State University, Department of Political Science, Public Administration Programs, 1974.

Cook, T. D., and Campbell, D. T. *Quasi-Experimentation: Design and Analysis Issues for Field Settings.* Chicago: Rand McNally, 1979.

Emlen, A., Lahti, J., Downs, G., McKay, A., and Downs, S. *Overcoming Barriers to Planning for Children in Foster Care.* Portland, Ore.: Portland State University, Regional Institute for Human Services, 1977.

Fast, D. A New Approach to Quantifying Training Program Effectiveness. *Training and Development Journal*, 1974, 28(9), 8–14.

Haynes, S. N. *Principles of Behavioral Assessment.* New York: Gardner, 1978.

Howard, G. S., Dailey, P. R., and Gulanick, N. A. The Feasibility of Informed Pre-tests in Attenuating Response Shift Bias. *Applied Psychological Measurement*, 1979, 3(4), 481–94.

Howard, G. S., Schmeck, R. R., and Bray, J. H. Internal Invalidity in Studies Employing Self-Report Instruments: A Suggested Remedy. *Journal of Educational Measurement*, 1979, 16(2), 129–35.

Locke, E. A., Shaw, K. N., Saari, L. M., and Latham, G. P. Goal Setting and Task Performance: 1969–1980. *Psychological Bulletin*, 1981, 90(1), 125–52.

Mezoff, B. *The Retrospective Shift: A Human Relations Training Phenomenon.* Amherst, Mass.: ODT Associates, 1979.

Mezoff, B. How to Get Accurate Self-Reports of Training Out-comes. *Training and Development Journal*, 1981, 35(9), 56–61.

Mosel, J. N. Why Training Programs Fail to Carry Over. *Personnel*, 1957, 33(3), 55–64.

Nunnally, J. C. *Psychometric Theory*. New York: McGraw Hill, 1978.

Oglesby, M. Paradigm for Evaluation of Training Programs for Community Mental Health. In M. Guttentag, T. Kiresuk, M. Oglesby, and J. Cahn, (Eds.), *The Evaluation of Training in Mental Health*. New York: Behavioral Pubns., 1975.

Petty, M. M., and Bruning, N. S. Relationships between Employee Training and Error Rates in Public Welfare Programs. *Administration in Social Work*, 1980, 4(1), 33–42.

Phillips, R. G. The Evolving Role of Modeling in the Management of Training. Paper presented at the ORSA/TIMS Joint National Meeting, San Juan, Puerto Rico, Paper, Oct. 1974.

Ralph, K. M. The Self-Report Response Shift Theory and NOW/THEN Self-Report Procedures. Doctoral dissertation, Southern Illinois University, 1975.

Schinke, S. P., Wong, S. E. Evaluation of Staff Training in Group Homes for Retarded Persons. *American Journal of Mental Deficiency*, 1977, 82(2), 130–36.

Schinke, S. P., and Wong, S. E. Teaching Child Care Workers: A Behavioral Approach. *Child Care Quarterly*, 1978, 7(1), 45–61.

Seppala, G. R. *An Approach to Determining the Value of Managerial Training*. Paper presented at the First Annual Invitational Research Seminar of the American Society for Training and Development, Pomona, Calif., Oct. 31–Nov. 2, 1978.

Stein, T. J., Gambrill, E. D., and Wilste, K. T. *Children in Foster Homes: Achieving Continuity of Care*. New York: Praeger, 1978.

Thomas, G., and LaCavera, A. *Evaluation Report—The West Virginia Department of Welfare Child Protective Services Training Project*. Athens, Ga.: Regional Institute for Social Welfare Research, 1981.

Urban Institute. *Developing Client Outcome Monitoring Systems: A Guide for State and Local Social Service Agencies*. Washington, D.C.: U.S. Department of Health and Human Services, Office of Human Development Services, 1981.

U.S. Office of Personnel Management. *Assessing Changes in Job Behaviors Due to Training: A Guide to the Participant Action Plan Ap-*

proach. Washington, D.C.: U.S. Government Printing Office, 1980. (Stock No. 006-000-01130-6)

Young, D. W., and Allen, B. Benefit-Cost Analysis in the Social Sciences: The Example of Adoption Reimbursement. *Social Science Review*, 1977, 51(2), 249–64.

Zober, M. A. Measuring the Effectiveness of In-Service Short-Term Training in a Human Service Setting: Introducing the Participant Action Plan Approach. Paper presented at the Evaluation Symposium, Cornell University, Department of Human Service Studies, Nov. 1980.

Zober, M. A., Seipel, M. D., and Skinner, V. Action-oriented Training and Evaluation: Motivating and Measuring Change in Job Performance as a Result of In-service Training in Departments of Social Service. *Journal of Continuing Social Work Education*, 1982, 2(1), 23–27.

Epilogue

WE REALIZE THAT THE REALITIES OF AGENCY LIFE MAY NOT always allow for a planned, rational approach to staff development program management. Consequently, the following guidelines are offered as a way of highlighting some workable compromises to managing and implementing staff development programs.

1. *Use of committees.* In scanning the many different roles presented in chapter 1, some managers may feel overwhelmed by the complexity and scope of staff development. While it may be difficult for one person to fulfill all the roles or possess all the skills, a committee of staff and consultants can be of substantial assistance in the planning, implementing, or evaluating of staff development activities. Besides providing technical advice, these committees can help build staff and managerial support for the eventual training. The involvement of line staff and supervisors in planning staff development activities is critical to the receptivity and success of staff development programs.

2. *Use of needs assessment and evaluation.* While many of the training-needs assessment and evaluation techniques described are surprisingly inexpensive to implement, many staff development personnel may lack the necessary time, expertise, or funds. Program crises occur, and unexpected training mandates have a way of appearing at the most inappropriate times. In these situations, emphasis should be placed on the design of job-relevant training using a select group of experienced workers, supervisors, and program man-

agers. Care should be taken to formulate specific and measurable learning objectives, even if the evaluation consists only of post-training participant ratings or the use of the PAPA technique. Attention paid "up-front" to job relevance and specific training objectives is essential for developing effective training programs. As Fine (1980) has noted, "In the end, any planning, managing, designing, evaluating, or policy decision is a lonely creative act based on incomplete information about past and present, an inadequate theory of cause and effect, an insufficient prediction of the future, and commonly disvalued subjective factors: personal knowledge and values" (p. 4). Planning committees can help to reduce those feelings of isolation and uncertainty of decision making that staff development managers experience.

3. *Use of training "consortia."* One of the most common problems of staff development personnel is lack of training funds. And yet some public and private agencies annually invite (at substantial expense) a renowned expert for several days of high quality training and fail to generate full enrollment. Funding such events sometimes reflects a lack of creative sharing of resources and expertise with other community agencies, and an opportunity to enhance program quality and stretch training dollars is lost. While organizational politics concerning contracts and funding may reduce agency cooperation, a training consortium can move beyond this barrier in order to maximize the effects of agency training funds.

4. *Use of expert in-house staff.* Even with adequate staff development funds, use of interagency training agreements or consortiums, and elaborate needs assessments hard decisions must be made regarding the trainers, learning objectives, and the level of difficulty

of the subject matter. While a regional or national reputation is a good indicator of trainer competence, trainers with relevant knowledge, experience, and training experience may already be on the agency's payroll or employed by a nearby agency. In-house staff might be able to address specific practice needs and present content at a level of difficulty that matches the audience's level of education, past training, and experience.

5. *Using alternatives to training sessions.* Too often staff development activities are limited to one to three day training sessions. Other methods exist to upgrade worker knowledge and skills such as temporary job reassignment, pairing of experienced and inexperienced staff (peer teaching), special forms of ongoing supervisory assistance, scheduled but informal brainstorming sessions, contracting for ethnic minority or other specialized case consultation, incorporating "journal clubs" into staff meetings where journal articles are presented, and distribution of readable policy or practice manuals from other agencies.

Organizations and workers need to be viewed as dynamic, objective learning systems. Attention must be paid to the values, beliefs, needs, and wants of workers at all levels, as well as to the current stage of organizational development and maturity. In this way, staff development planning can take into account the life cycle stages and current functioning of both the organization and the staff. For example, how will staff development programs affect organizational goals? What kinds of training activities are appropriate for new, old, or self-renewing organizations? Will training activities alter job performance in one section or program while hindering job performance in another? In other words, it is important to assess the different effects of staff development programs on various persons and groups as well as on the capacity and productivity of the organization as a whole. This form of assessment involves predicting what workers will need to know in order to implement policies or programs as well as predicting what training methods will be most useful and efficient in meeting those needs. According to Fine (1980), staff development managers must please many different types of people with different interests, wants, and needs:

> In addition to having to please the administrator who has the power to approve or deny budget requests, (s)he must also please peer level managers and supervisors, gatekeepers, who make specific training requests and who approve the participation of particular workers. The workers who participate in training have to be pleased—they complain, criticize and boycott training sessions. People who provide support services have to be pleased, at least enough to secure their cooperation. Each of the different types of persons and interest enclaves has a different stake in training. Each sees costs and benefits differently. Each judges training on how well it seems to satisfy their own role and work requirements. [P. 24]

Maintaining programs and retaining adequate numbers of staff tend to be high administrative priorities, and sometimes staff development programs are relegated to a back-seat position. Thus, staff development personnel must be prepared and willing to advocate for staff development program survival. One strategy is to monitor staff performance reviews and program audits that may highlight service delivery issues and training needs. Another strategy is to use the results of well-designed training evaluations as evidence of the positive value of training programs.

Skillful staff development managers also view training as an important component of various program innovations. For example, a state child welfare agency began a system of intensive in-home casework services to prevent foster care placement. In this case, the redeployment of staff and reorganization of services included specialized training as part of the program redesign activities. Proactive staff development managers bring to the job a sense of organizational priorities, political realities, and program creativity which enable them to design staff training in connection with new or improved services.

The management of staff development programs is an essential ingredient of a progressive organization and requires the use of a wide variety of technical, interpersonal, and political skills. It is important that personnel involved in staff development program management understand all of the important concepts and techniques in order to handle the periodic feelings of being overwhelmed. We hope that this book has provided a new perspective of staff development program management as well as some additional tools with which to improve organizational life.

Reference

Fine, J. *Planning and Assessing Agency Training.* Washington, D.C.: U.S. Department of Health, Education, and Welfare, 1980.

Appendices

Appendix A
Implementor's Checklist

Title of Workshop _____

Month and day(s) _____

Hour(s) _____

Sponsor(s) _____

Location (name of building, hotel, rooms, etc.) _____

Intended audience (names of organizations, professions, general
public, etc.) _____

Size of audience expected _____

Brief outline of program

Title of individual section	Individual responsible	Phone no.

Fees for participants

Regular $_____ Student $_____ Senior citizen $_____

Part-time attendees, if allowed $_____

Transportation available to site (air, bus, limousine, etc.)
_____

Will participants need a map?   Yes _____   No _____

Who will provide?_____

FACILITIES

Meeting room reserved (give name, number, capacity of each, equipment desired in each, set-up desired—classroom style etc.— charge for each, and other relevant information). Some facilities provide you with a floor plan. _____

_____

_____

_____

_____

_____

If appropriate, draw a diagram of each room, giving approximate dimensions, location of exits, thermostats, light switches, etc. Hotels may give you hospitality rooms (indicate names or room numbers, location, number of people each will accommodate, hours reserved, charges and other relevant details). _____

_____

_____

_____

_____

Overnight accommodations

How many rooms are reserved for your group? _____
What date will hotel release them to others? _____
What are charges? Single _____ Double _____
Suite _____ Other _____
Who is responsible for notifying hotel of reservations?
Participants _____
Committee member (name) _____
Phone number _____
For which speakers are you providing overnight accommodations?

_____

_____

_____

Name of individual at hotel to contact regarding overnight accommodations:
_____ Phone _____
Names of auxiliary facilities, if needed (hotel, restaurants, etc.)

_____

_____

Parking
Where located _____
Charges, if any _____
Permits, coupons, etc. needed and where available _____
_____

Other Facilities (Indicate location and other pertinent facts)
Entrances _____
Exits _____
Handicap facilities _____
Loading areas _____
Bus, airline, or limousine pickup areas _____
_____
Rest rooms _____
_____
Public telephones _____
_____
First aid stations _____
Message center _____
Public stenographer _____
Restriction on use of buildings or rooms (describe) _____
_____
News stands and gift shops _____
_____
Display areas _____

EQUIPMENT AND SUPPLIES

Item: Check those needed   To be provided by

Slide projector   _____   _____
Overhead projector   _____   _____
Screen   _____   _____
Tape recorder   _____   _____
Tape cassettes   _____   _____
Film projector   _____   _____
Films (give titles)   _____   _____
                              _____   _____
Camera   _____   _____
Microphones: table   _____   _____
              lavaliere   _____   _____
Extension cords   _____   _____
Telephone(s)   _____   _____
Blackboards/
   chalk/erasers   _____   _____

Curtains (to
   darken rooms)   _____   _____
Easels/easel paper   _____   _____
Pointers   _____   _____
Cash box   _____   _____
Money (how much?)   _____   _____
Registration tables   _____   _____
Message board   _____   _____
Name tags   _____   _____
Pencils   _____   _____
Pens   _____   _____
Pads of paper   _____   _____
Tape   _____   _____
Scissors   _____   _____
Pins   _____   _____
Thumbtacks   _____   _____
Receipt books   _____   _____
Meal tickets   _____   _____
Ashtrays   _____   _____
Water pitchers/glasses   _____   _____
Display tables   _____   _____
Dollies   _____   _____
Coat racks   _____   _____
Other supplies   _____   _____

Special personnel needed (Give names and phone numbers)
Registration personnel_____
Equipment operators_____
Other_____

PUBLICITY/PRINTED MATERIALS NEEDED

Item   To be provided by

Advance announcements _____
   Date needed _____
   Approximate cost $_____

Follow-up flier _____
   Date needed _____
   Approximate cost $_____

Program _____
   Date needed _____
   Approximate cost $_____

Evaluation form _____

Date needed _____
Approximate cost $_____
To be analyzed by _____
To be distributed to _____

Copies of speakers' presentations

Date needed _____
Approximate cost $_____
To be submitted to _____

Proceedings or summary report

Date needed _____
Approximate cost _____
To be distributed to _____
Charge to participants, if any $_____
To others $_____

News release

Date needed _____
Approximate cost $_____
To be distributed to _____

Other materials (posters, listing in special calendars, etc.) Describe

_____

_____

Date needed _____
Approximate cost $_____
Mailing lists (list those to be used and indicate who will be responsible for each as well as form in which they exist and
charges involved.) _____

_____

_____

MEAL ARRANGEMENTS

Breakfasts

Time and place	Charge	Tax	Tip	Ticket needed?	Guarantee date	Contact person
1.						
2.						
3.						
4.						

Indicate menus if desired:

1. _____
2. _____
3. _____
4. _____

Lunches

Time and place	Charge	Tax	Tip	Ticket needed?	Guarantee date	Contact person

1. _____
2. _____
3. _____
4. _____

Indicate menus if desired:

1. _____
2. _____
3. _____
4. _____

Dinners

Time and place	Charge	Tax	Tip	Ticket needed?	Guarantee date	Contact person

1. _____
2. _____
3. _____
4. _____

Indicate menus if desired:

1. _____
2. _____
3. _____
4. _____

Coffee breaks and/or receptions

Time and place	Charge	Tax	Tip	Ticket needed?	Guarantee date	Contact person
1.						
2.						
3.						
4.						
5.						
6.						
7.						
8.						
9.						
10.						
11.						
12.						

Adapted from Carol B. Ovens, *Taking the "Work" out of Workshops* (Seattle, Wash.: Division of Marine Resources, University of Washington, 1980).

Appendix B
A Self-Assessment Inventory for Managing A Staff Development Program

This inventory represents an effort to model the process of learner readiness. Are you ready? If your answers indicate that you can adequately perform all the items noted in the inventory, then this book should be a useful refresher. If you feel unsure about your understanding of the items and your capacity to carry them out on the job, then this book should prove to be very useful. You can use the inventory twice, before and after reading the chapters, by simply covering up your first set of answers. Remember that not all the items are addressed in the book but most of them are described.

I. SKILLS RELATED TO THE ORGANIZATION

	Self-Assessment		
	Need to do it better	Doing all right	Do it very effectively
1. I am able to state my organization's aims as described by management.			
2. I maintain an up-to-date knowledge of learning needs in my organization as seen by management and staff.			
3. I can describe the dynamics of change in my organization.			
4. I recognize changes that could lead to future learning needs.			

Self-Assessment

	Need to do it better	Doing all right	Do it very effectively
5. I can describe the *formal* and *informal* patterns of authority and responsibility in my organization.			
6. I can influence the decisions about what resources are allocated to training.			
7. I can establish cooperative working relationships with my associates.			
8. I can describe the mood of a work group as it relates to accomplishing tasks (for example: tense/relaxed? guarded/open? hostile/jovial? productive/blocked?).			
9. I can define the boundaries of my work (for example: my authority, my responsibility).			
10. I can list tasks to be accomplished by other staff in preparation for training.			
11. I can describe the effects of training on the organization in which I work.			
12. I can identify the training implications of new legislation.			
13. I have current knowledge of how staff view training.			
14. I can identify training needs which emerge from organizational problems and activities.			

II. SKILLS RELATED TO ANALYZING PREVIOUS TRAINING ACTIVITIES

	Self-Assessment		
	Need to do it better	Doing all right	Do it very effectively
15. I can describe staff who have participated in previous training (for example: numbers, jobs held, levels of experience, location in organization).			
16. I can obtain and assess formal evaluation data of previous training.			
17. I can collect informal evaluative data about previous training (for example: by using files, discussions with participants and management, examining materials/training design).			
18. I can assess effectiveness of the instructional methods used in previous training.			
19. I can relate the content covered in previous training events to content proposed for future events.			
20. I can describe points of potential resistance by participants to proposed content.			
21. I can create strategies to assist participants in reducing their resistance to learning.			

III. SKILLS RELATED TO DEVELOPING OBJECTIVES

Self-Assessment

	Need to do it better	Doing all right	Do it very effectively
22. I can describe the target participants for the training event I am planning (for example: jobs held, levels of experience, location in organization, numbers).			
23. I can distinguish between organizational needs that can be solved by training and organizational needs for which training is not an appropriate solution.			
24. I can identify training needs as seen by staff and management through the use of several needs assessment techniques.			
25. I can translate training needs into written training objectives.			
26. I can involve all levels of the organization in establishing learning objectives.			
27. I can write achievable, job-performance-based learning objectives that can be understood by the target audience.			
28. I can identify a set of realistic learning objectives given the limits of available resources.			

Self-Assessment

	Need to do it better	Doing all right	Do it very effectively
29. Given a set of learning objectives, I can establish criteria for the selection of internal and external people to lead a training event (for example: consultants, trainers, and support staff).			

IV. SKILLS RELATED TO DEVELOPING LEARNING ACTIVITIES

Self-Assessment

	Need to do it better	Doing all right	Do it very effectively
30. I can contract with consultants of staff trainers to assist in design preparation.			
31. I can apply adult learning principles in designing training events based on learning objectives.			
32. I can match predesigned learning activities (for example: from off-the-shelf programs, from publications) with the learning objectives for this event.			
33. I can select a manageable amount of content for a given activity.			

	Self-Assessment		
	Need to do it better	Doing all right	Do it very effectively
34. I can select, adapt, and mix learning methods (for example: lecture, film, skill practice) appropriate for each learning objective's content.			
35. I can guard against information overload when a great deal of data must be communicated.			
36. I can recognize when it is time for a group to take a break.			
37. I can get ongoing feedback from the participants in a training event.			
38. I am receptive to personal feedback from participants.			
39. I can assess the effects of my behavior on participants.			

V. Skills Related to Gathering Resources

	Self-Assessment		
	Need to do it better	Doing all right	Do it very effectively
40. I gather information about participating staff and their skill levels in proposed training content.			

Self-Assessment

	Need to do it better	Doing all right	Do it very effectively
41. I can compile the content matter needed to meet selected learning objectives.			
42. I can evaluate appropriate training media and materials to support the learning activities.			
43. I can set up for events (for example: arrange furniture, order materials, procure needed audiovisual equipment, arrange for snacks).			
44. I can access resources (for example: printing, audiovisual production) within and outside my organization.			
45. I can negotiate contracts for staff, facilities, and materials for training events.			
46. I can prepare a budget for training events.			

VI. SKILLS RELATED TO SCHEDULING

Self-Assessment

	Need to do it better	Doing all right	Do it very effectively
47. I am able to develop and work on short-range and long-range schedules.			

Self-Assessment

	Need to do it better	Doing all right	Do it very effectively
48. I can schedule tasks and activities in an appropriate sequence.			
49. I can establish tasks for participants to do in preparation for training events.			
50. I can maintain a current written project schedule on the status of preparations for a training event.			
51. I can establish tasks for myself with clear completion goals.			
52. I can balance the time involved in preparation for training events with my other job assignments.			
53. I can work well under pressure (for example: time, energy, supervisor, personal life).			

VII. Skills Related to Participant Recruitment

Self-Assessment

	Need to do it better	Doing all right	Do it very effectively
54. I can define the audience to be trainers in market terms (who wants or needs this training?).			

Self-Assessment

	Need to do it better	Doing all right	Do it very effectively
55. I can describe training content to be covered in easily understood promotional materials (for example: verbal, handwritten, brochure, poster, newsletter).			
56. I can obtain feedback on the accuracy and impact of the promotional materials.			
57. I can develop strategies to disseminate promotional materials to all potential participants.			
58. I can influence people in the organization to reinforce the promotional message (for example: persuade? recommend? coerce? reward? invite?).			

VIII. SKILLS RELATED TO TRAINING PROGRAM EVALUATION

Self-Assessment

	Need to do it better	Doing all right	Do it very effectively
59. I can construct practical means for measuring participants' *skills* before and after the training event.			
60. I can construct practical means for measuring participants' *knowledge* before and after the training event.			

Self-Assessment

	Need to do it better	Doing all right	Do it very effectively
61. I can construct practical means for measuring participants' work-related *attitudes* before and after the training event.			
62. I can measure the degree to which management's expectations of this training event were fulfilled.			
63. I can measure the degree to which participants' expectations of this training event were fulfilled.			
64. I know the difference between process and outcome evaluation.			
65. I can use the evaluation data from a training event to help plan future training events.			
66. I can measure costs versus benefits of a training event.			
67. I can report training results to participants and management in an appropriate format.			
68. I can design follow-up activities to reinforce the learnings of participants after the training event.			

Adapted from Stephen F. Sauer and Ronald E. Holland, *Planning In-House Training* (San Diego, Calif.: University Associates, 1981).

Appendix C
Learning Objectives
Self-Assessment Exercise
(To be completed after reading chapter 5)

One way to test one's skill in developing learning objectives is to engage in self-assessment. The first set of items tests one's ability to evaluate a learning objective in terms of its performance orientation. Does it tell what the worker will be doing when demonstrating his or her achievement of the objective? Take a moment and complete the first part of this exercise. After you have completed part 1, complete part 2, where the appropriate columns should be checked if the characteristics of performance, condition, and criterion can be located in each sample learning objective (i.e., mark each of these characteristics as they are present in the learning objective). Performance refers to the action or activity behaviors in the learning objective, usually reflected in an action verb. Condition refers to the situation or context in which the learning is to be applied. Criterion refers to the quality or outcome expected of the learned behavior, usually reflected in such adjectives as comprehensive, coherent, and complete. The answers are noted at the end of the exercise.

PART 1

	Does it state a performance?	
	Yes	No
1. Be able to understand the principles of counseling	____	____
2. Be able to write three examples of the relationships between human behavior and social environment.	____	____
3. Understand the meaning of client confidentiality.	____	____
4. Be able to name major components of a social history.	____	____

5. Be able to recognize the needs for child care associated with child abuse and neglect. ____ ____

6. Be able to really understand the writings of Freud. ____ ____

7. Be able to identify (circle) objectives that include a statement of desired performance. ____ ____

8. Be able to recognize that the practical application of interviewing skills requires time and experience. ____ ____

9. Be able to appreciate the ability of others and engage in group process. ____ ____

10. Be able to describe the major uses of a client information system. ____ ____

PART 2

	PER- FORMANCE	CON- DITION	CRI- TERION
11. Be able to demonstrate a knowledge of the principles of counseling.	____	____	____
12. Be able to write a complete social history.	____	____	____
13. Using agency manuals, be able to name every item needed on the client intake form.	____	____	____
14. Be able to write a description of the steps involved in completing a client discharge form.	____	____	____
15. Using agency equipment, be able to complete a dictation of client progress notes within ten minutes following standard recording form.	____	____	____
16. Know well the code of ethics which guides the profession.	____	____	____
17. Given an oral description of the case review process, be able to complete peer review forms.	____	____	____
18. Be able to write a coherent press release, using agency reports, on the success of the crisis hotline.	____	____	____
19. Be able to develop logical approaches to the solution of staff communication problems.	____	____	____

20. Without reference materials, be able to describe three approaches to treating clients reflected in most community mental health programs. _____ _____ _____

Answers for Learning Objectives Self-Assessment Parts I and II

PART I

1. No
2. Yes "Write"
3. No
4. Yes "Name"
5. No

6. No
7. Yes "Identify and circle"
8. No
9. No
10. Yes "Describe"

PART 2

	PERFORMANCE	CONDITION	CRITERION
11.			
12.	X		
13.	X	X	X
14.	X		
15.	X	X	X
16.			
17.	X	X	
18.	X	X	
19.			
20.	X	X	X

How did you do? Do you disagree with any of the answers?

Appendix D
Guide to Writing a Description of an Instructional Program

TITLE
Title as given in the bulletin or announcement (be specific).

> *Example:* Introduction to Behavior Change Theories for Family Therapy

FOR
Indicate who can take the course and prerequisites if any.

> *Example:* Open to social caseworkers, psychiatrists, and clinical psychologists who are currently carrying at least one family in their caseloads. Previous work in behavior modification is not necessary.

COURSE OVERVIEW
A one- or two-sentence statement is sufficient. It is stated from the program's point of view, and is descriptive in nature.

> *Example:* The course is designed to give mental health technicians an overview of behavior change theories and to examine selected applications of their practice. Theories covered will include those of Freudian psychologists, behavioral psychologists, social psychologists, and Lewinian field theorists. The implications of various theoretical approaches for case finding, referral, and treatment will be explored.

PERFORMANCE OBJECTIVES
Performance objectives are written for use by the participant and the instructor, but they are about the participant. They specify to the instructor what is to be taught and to the participant what she or he is expected to learn or be able to do on completion of the course. In designing a set of course objectives, the instructor might ask himself or herself the following question: What kinds of things should the participant be able to do at the end of this course (within the confines of the overall course description, item 2) that will most

effectively help the participant become a more skilled human services worker in the least amount of time?

Other questions might relate to knowledge and attitude or value change, career mobility, and the functional requirements of the participant's occupation or work situation.

Course objectives should be written in a manner that clearly communicates the instructional intent. The instructional intent should be specified in behavioral terms; that is, it should communicate what the participant will be doing when demonstrating achievement.

A well-designed performance objective will identify and name a learning activity that includes specified outcomes and the criterion for acceptable performance.

> *Example:* The participant must be able to specify in 200 to 400 words the eight stages in human development discussed by Erikson and must give three or four examples from the literature of how arrested development at an earlier level may result in inappropriate or harmful behavior in the last three stages.

> *Example:* The participant will be able to prepare an analysis of any three of the ten cases given him or her in a final examination. The analysis must clearly relate to the concepts and principles covered in five workshops (reference must be made to at least five shop sessions and/or reading assignments in substantiating the analysis). In each case, however, the analysis must indicate consideration of two or more points of view (from the literature or group discussions) and must be stated in the participant's own words. References and notes may be used, and up to one week may be taken for completion of the assignment.

> *Example:* The participant will design a proposal for funding a new mental health service and locate at least one funding source likely to show interest in the proposal.

All the relevant course objectives should be listed. Note that it is possible to develop subobjectives for each of those given above. Also, each instructor may design a set of learning objectives for each learning episode, i.e., for each lecture, exercise, or reading assignment during the course. It is not necessary to list all of these in this space. They can be distributed to participants at the end of the preceding session or at the session for which the objectives are designed. There may, in fact, be times in which the writer will include objectives that are not fully behaviorally specific. She or he may not know until teaching the course or leading the seminar once, for example, what can realistically be expected from participants. Nevertheless, the more specific the objective, the fairer to the participant, the better a guide it is to the instructor, and the easier it is to redesign. The following principles may serve as a guide to the designer:

1. The objective must say something about the participant and what is expected of her or him, not about the instructor, the kind of classroom experience participants will have, or about the textbook and other teaching materials.
2. The objective is about ends rather than means. It specifies what the participant should be able to do—the expected terminal behavior—rather than the course content or the performance of the instructor.
3. Properly designed, the objective should also specify under what conditions the participant will demonstrate the terminal behavior: in an examination, a termpaper, a problem-solving exercise conducted in the classroom or at work, an observation in the field, a counseling session with a client, an oral report in the classroom, etc.
4. An instructional objective may also include information about the level of performance that will be considered acceptable, for example, "three of the ten cases," "five or six major components," "three or four examples from the literature" (see examples given above) or "at least 80 percent correct replies in the self-assessment questionnaire."

It is possible to classify objectives into (1) those that specify greater knowledge or information; (2) those that specify performance skills; and (3) those that specify maturation, attitude change, or greater independence. The instructor must be careful not to judge the participant on the basis of one criterion when another set of objectives was specified. Thus if an ability to work independently (or cooperatively) is a desired outcome of the course, this should be specified and the terminal behavior noted.

Please note that objectives need not be static. They can be modified as experience shows them to be unrealistic (too easily achieved or too difficult to accomplish), as experience through outside analysis reveals gaps, as participants and instructors jointly agree they must be modified, or as overall curriculum considerations require.

Once defined, objectives can also help determine the behavioral competence required of participants prior to entry into a course or program of instruction. The objectives found on each course description can be used in the establishment of entry criteria (prereq-uisites) for that course and thus of the expected terminal behavior of participants in the courses that precede or accompany the course in question. A fully integrated curriculum requires that as the objectives in one course shift or as their achievement varies, the objectives of other courses will be modified. For this reason the written statement should be viewed as tentative and subject to re-view and rewriting. It is a beginning contribution to the design of an integrated and more comprehensive curriculum.

Specification of objectives will also make the instructor's task of describing content, course requirements, and format a great deal easier.

CONTENT DESCRIPTION

This section may be written in a number of different ways. The fol-lowing lists some of the more traditional ways of describing course content:

List of topics for each session.
Description of content organized into study units.
Abstract of overall content, much as one might write an abstract of a book or article.
Description of the content in relationship to each of the course objective.

PRINCIPAL TEXTS AND READING ASSIGNMENTS

If one or more texts or readers are to be used, list them here. The name of the author and relevant articles or books may be listed in detail in this section. Alternatively, reference can be made to a bibli-ography with only the author or number on the bibliography listed here.

Example: Mager, Robert F., Preparing Educational Objec-tives. Palo Alto, Calif.: Fearson, 1962.

Example: See Bibliography.
Mager (62); Bass and Vaughan (66); McGehee and Thayer (61).

Example: See Bibliography.
Educational Objectives: Mager.
Management Training: Bass and Vaughan, chaps. 1 and 2.
Vocational Instruction: McGehee and Thayer, chaps. 2, 3, and 5.

Roleplay: Workers roleplay or act-out the roles of assigned char-acters. This may be impromptu, as when the "actor" decides on the words and actions, or prescribed, as when the words and actions are predetermined, usually written on a handout for the actor to follow.

REQUIREMENTS

This section should relate closely to the three preceding sections, especially the performance objectives. Requirements should be as specific as possible. Participants should know what is expected of them. Some categories of expectations include:

Attendance required
Participation (sharing ideas in class or contributing to class development).
Extent to which the participant should be independent or autonomous in choice of learning objective, content or approach to learning, and communication of what he or she has learned.
Specify all assignments in this section.
Reports or special projects.

FORMAT

The major categories in this area are course, seminar, laboratory, workshop, reading course or independent study, and practicum. Within these categories, a number of methods and teaching and learning techniques are possible. These include case studies, lectures, simulations, programmed instruction, role playing, small-group problem solving, in-basket techniques, structured field experience, etc. If the format and teaching approach is a central feature of the learning experience, it should be described in some detail.

Example: The entire seminar will revolve around the analysis and development of case studies. During the first four sessions, students will read and analyze selected cases at home for discussion in the classroom. Role playing may be used to examine alternative intervention approaches and to simulate the processes of case consultation and case conferences.

The next two sessions will include a lecture presentation plus several didactic exercises aimed at preparing students for development of their own cases for sharing and analysis. The last four sections will be devoted to participant presentations.

RELATIONSHIPS TO OTHER PROGRAMS

The relationship between this activity and other staff development programs should be made explicit (if they are relevant):

Other courses or activities for which this one may be a prerequisite.

Other courses or activities that must (or should) be taken concurrently.

Specific relationships to content or experiences in other courses (e.g., "An advanced approach to the use of simulations and role playing, which will give the student an opportunity to build on previous experiences in his or her work setting").

What differentiates this course or activity from others (e.g., "This is one of the few opportunities for psychologists in the school system to do advanced work in . . .").

In addition, the workshop or activity may be of specific relevance to the learners' occupational, professional, or career interests.

Example: The nature of the issues to be discussed will help participants to identify their personal value systems and to contrast their reward-value hierarchies with the accepted values of their professions.

Example: The content is particularly relevant to those mental health professionals who are currently working or who anticipate working with children and youth from disadvantaged backgrounds.

Example: Unit 2 of the seminar is of special interest to nurses who are currently or expect soon to be in supervisory positions.

BIBILIOGRAPHY

This section should be as thorough and complete as it is on any well-designed course outline: "short enough to be interesting but long enough to cover the ground."

Appendix E
Training Techniques

The following list of techniques is by no means exhaustive, and you are encouraged to expand your repertoire by observing training models, researching, and creating your own techniques.

Use of experts: An expert is anyone who has a special talent, skill, or background. Experts may be called upon to lecture and to demonstrate creative activities whenever the topic requires specialized knowledge or skills (for example, a child psychologist, an attorney, a doctor). The use of experts lends variety to the training and establishes credibility.

Lecture, mini-lecture: Lectures are useful when it is important to establish a common body of knowledge and common understandings among the participants as a foundation for more active experiences. Mini-lectures are incorporated into the training process when factual information must be established prior to discussion or other participatory exercises.

Group discussion: Discussions may be structured or unstructured. You may use questions, experiential exercises, worksheets, case studies, etc., to structure group discussion. Unstructured group discussions frequently arise spontaneously and require little prompting. In either type of group discussion, it is important for you to maintain an atmosphere of openness and trust and to be accepting and reinforcing. You must also encourage participation from all members and prevent the dominance of any one member. You should frequently redirect questions, clarify what has been said, and summarize the major points.

Experiential exercise: Exercises that require active involvement and the application of personal experiences are most conducive to adult learning. These exercises provide the workers with opportunities to apply content, to test hypotheses, to practice skills, to arrive at creative solutions and to explore personal values and attitudes. These activities facilitate group skills such as cooperation and the ability to reach consensus. In this type of exercise, workers are guided by the task rather than by the trainer. Experiential exercises most strongly support the principle that the most valuable learning is an autonomous act. In addition, these exercises are often the most interesting and the most fun.

Some experiential exercises are brief while others require lengthy processing. For example, a warm-up exercise that is designed to help participants get acquainted may take no longer than fifteen minutes, whereas case study activities are scheduled for one hour. The following are common experiential exercises.

Roleplay: Workers role play or act-out the roles of assigned characters. This may be impromptu, as when the "actor" decides on the words and actions, or prescribed, as when the words and actions are predetermined, usually written on a handout for the actor to follow.

Worksheets: Worksheets often serve to provide practice in a particular exercise (a series of directions), to provide reinforcement for content (an outline), to direct an experiential activity (a consensus value judgment exercise), or to gather information (a questionnaire).

In-basket: A worksheet with a series of directions or questions, role play assignments, special directions, etc., may be folded and placed "in a basket," and randomly selected by members of the group. This technique avoids specific assignments, is quiet, and protects secrecy when it is necessary, as it is in some role play or charade situations.

Case studies: Written case studies are used to stimulate discussion, encourage problem-solving, explore value judgments, and foster the exchange of experiences.

Value judgments and rank ordering: Worksheets or oral exercises that involve rank ordering and prioritizing, such as the familiar question, "Who would you save if you had room for only three on a life boat?" encourage group discussion and give practice in compromise and reaching consensus.

Critical incidence solutions: Actual incidences that are relevant to the trainees' situations are best used to stimulate discussion, explore alternatives, share experiences, and evaluate possible solutions.

Problem solving: Specific problems may be described to a training group to initiate discussion. This usually stimulates the group to define and seek solutions for actual problems encountered in their work.

Guided imagery: An effective method of changing pace, of relaxing participants, and of encouraging quiet self-exploration is guided imagery, which involves directing the group to relax, close their eyes, and imagine a place for a situation that the trainer describes.

Checklist: Checklists may be used to gather information on the group, evaluate training, identify specific interests, evaluate performance, afford opportunity to practice what has been learned, and strengthen recall.

Adapted from *The Leader's Manual: Supplement to Virginia Day Care Skills Training Guide,* by Patricia Bell, Kathryn Bell, Ann Gardner, and Marilyn Levie. (Richmond, Va.: TAPP Ass., 1980), pp. 35–38.

References

American Society for Training and Development. *Professional Development: A Self-Development Process for Training and Development Professionals.* Madison, Wis.: American Society for Training and Development, 1979.

American Society for Training and Development. *Training and Development Handbook* (2d ed.) edited by Robert L. Craig. New York: McGraw-Hill, 1976.

Anderson, Ronald H. *Selecting and Developing Media for Instruction.* New York: Van Nostrand Reinhold, 1976.

Bell, Patricia, Kathryn Bell, Ann Gardner, and Marilyn Levie. *The Leader's Manual: Supplement to Virginia Day Care Skills Training Guide.* Richmond, Va.: TAPP Assoc., 1980.

Benne, Kenneth D., Leland P. Bradford, Jack R. Gibb, and Ronald D. Lippitt. *The Laboratory Method of Changing and Learning.* Palo Alto, Calif.: Science and Behavior Books, 1975.

Bliss, Edwin C. *Getting Things Done.* New York: Bantam Books. 1976.

Bormann, Ernest G., and Nancy C. Bormann. *Effective Small Group Communication.* Minneapolis, Minn.: Burgess Pub. Co., 1976.

Brown, F. Gerald, and Kenneth R. Wedel. *Assessing Training Needs.* Washington, D.C.: National Training and Development Service Press, 1974.

Burke, W. Warner, and Richard Beckhard. *Conference Planning* (2d ed.). San Diego, Calif.: University Associates, 1976.

Cinnamon, Kenneth M. et al. *Applied Skills Training Series* (5vols.). St. Louis, Mo.: Applied Skills Press, 1979–1981.

Davis, Larry N. *Planning-Conducting-Evaluating Workshops.* Austin, Tex.: Learning Concepts, 1974.

Donaldson, Les, and Edward E. Scannel. *Human Resource Develop-*

ment: The New Trainer's Guide. Reading, Mass.: Addison-Wesley, 1978.

Dyer, William G. (Ed.). *Modern Theory and Method in Group Training.* New York: Van Nostrand Reinhold, 1972.

Forbess-Green, Sue. *The Encyclopedia of Icebreakers.* St. Louis, Mo.: Applied Skills Press, 1981.

George, James E., and Earl L. McCallon. *Planning a Competency-Based Staff Development Program.* Hingham, Mass.: Teaching Resources, 1976.

Kaufman, Roger. *Identifying and Solving Problems.* San Diego, Calif.: University Associates, 1976.

Knowles, Malcolm S. *The Adult Learner: A Neglected Species* (2d ed.). Houston: Gulf Pub. Co., 1978.

Knowles, Malcolm S. *The Modern Practice of Adult Education.* New York: Association Press, 1970.

Koberg, Don, and Jim Bagnall. *The Universal Traveler: A Soft-Systems Guide to Creativity, Problem Solving, and the Process of Reaching Goals.* Los Altos, Calif.: William Kaufman, 1976.

Laird, Dugan. *Approaches to Training and Development.* Reading, Mass.: Addison-Wesley, 1978.

Lauffer, Armand. *Doing Continuing Education and Staff Development.* New York: McGraw-Hill, 1978.

Mager, Robert F. *Preparing Instructional Objectives* (2d ed.). Belmont, Calif.: Fearon Pub., 1975.

Mager, Robert F., and Peter Pipe. *Analyzing Performance Problems or "You Really Oughta Wanna."* Belmont, Calif,: Fearon Pub., 1972.

Margolis, Fredric H. *Training by Objectives.* Cambridge, Mass.: McBer & Co., 1970.

McKim, Robert H. *Experiences in Visual Thinking.* Monterey, Calif.: Brooks/Cole, 1972.

McLagan, Patricia A. *Helping Others Learn: Designing Programs for Adults.* Reading, Mass.: Addison/Wesley, 1978.

Miles, Matthew B. *Learning to Work in Groups.* New York: Teachers College Press, Columbia University, 1973.

Mill, Cyril R. *Activities for Trainers: 50 Useful Designs*. San Diego: University Associates, 1980.

Morris, Kenneth T., and Kenneth M. Cinnamon. *A Handbook of Verbal Group Exercises*. St. Louis, Mo.: CMA Pub. Co., 1974.

Nadler, Leonard. *Developing Human Resources* (2d ed.). Austin, Tex.: Learning Concepts, 1979.

Nadler, Leonard, and Zeace Nadler. *The Conference Book*. Houston, Tex.: Gulf Pub. Co., 1977.

Odiorne, George S. *Training by Objectives: An Economic Approach to Management Training*. New York: Macmillan, 1970.

Pfeiffer, J. William, and John E. Jones (Eds.). *The Annual Handbooks for Group Facilitators* (10 vols.). San Diego, Calif.: University Associates, 1972–1981.

Pfeiffer, J. William, and John E. Jones (Eds.). *A Handbook of Structured Experiences for Human Relations Training* (8 vols.). San Diego, Calif.: University Associates, 1973–1981.

Pfeiffer, J. William, and John E. Jones (Eds.). *Reference Guide to Handbooks and Annuals* (rev. ed.). San Diego, Calif.: University Associates, 1981.

This, Leslie E. *The Small Meeting Planner*. Houston, Tex.: Gulf Pub. Co., 1971.

Torshen, Kay. *The Mastery Approach to Competency-Based Education*. New York: Academic Press, 1977.

Weiss, C. H. *Evaluation Research: Methods for Assessing Program Effectiveness*. Englewood Cliffs, N.J.: Prentice-Hall, 1972.

Wexley, Kenneth N., and Gary P. Latham. *Developing and Training Human Resources in Organization*. Glenview, Ill.: Scott, Foresman, 1981.

Zemke, Ronald. *Figuring Things Out: A Guide to Task Analysis*. Reading, Mass.: Addison-Wesley, 1982.

Index